IT'S POSSIBLE

NEVER UNDERESTIMATE YOURSELF

BEATRICE WILLIAMSON

White Blackbird
BOOKS

Bea Williamson is an inspiration to so many for her phenomenal leadership of the Maisha program. In this little book, she shares her scriptural touchstones and insights for rising above one's most difficult circumstances. The aim of the author is authentic and clear. By sharing her hope with others, readers will soon realize that she is a real person with a real story who they can hold on to in overcoming their own struggles.

Ann T. Riley
PhD, Clinical Assistant Professor, University of Oklahoma Anne & Henry School of Social Work

DEDICATION

This book is dedicated to everyone who is going through challenges in life. You are facing what seems impossible, but I want you to know that the

IMPOSSIBLE
is possible

for everyone who has the courage to pursue their dreams.

I think anything is possible if you have the mindset and the will and desire to do it and put the time in.

—Roger Clemens

CONTENTS

ACKNOWLEDGEMENTS

I would like to thank the Almighty God for always guiding me and giving me the courage to write. You have helped in me many unexplainable ways to make the impossible possible.

For these dearest ones, thank you seems so insufficient, yet I humbly offer my deepest gratitude to—

My incredible children at Maisha. Thank you for making me a mother and for the gift that each one of you and each moment spent with you. Thank you for willing to share your life with me and the opportunity to serve you.

Grandma in heaven, mom, and all my family members both Kenya and in the United States—thank you for believing in me, no matter what, for always pushing me to follow my dreams, and for dreaming with me. Mom, you taught me how to love unconditionally and how to live with kindness, strength, joy, and grace. You have been my strong shoulder and greatest encourager. I am proud to call you mama and share you with our community in Kano, in Kisumu, Kenya. Thank you for your support and prayers to make this work a reality.

Doug and Mije, thank you for pouring your time and heart into this book and encouraging me. This book is a reality because of you. What a precious gift from God that he put you in my life for such a time like this. And to all my mentors, thank you for the opportunity to learn and drink from the oases of your wisdom. You inspire me beyond words.

To the Maisha Project team and all the volunteers around the world—your love, encouragement, and support inspires me to do much more. The work of Maisha is not just a great achievement of one person. It has been inspired by many. I sincerely say *asante sana* to you.

Ann, AJ, and McAfee—thank you for reading this manuscript long before it was a book and believing it could be. Thank you for all the advice and wisdom. You are three of the greatest gifts God graced me with. Thank you for being my friends through thick or thin.

My Yahweh created all of this. My thank you is so minuscule to express my gratitude to you. Thank you to trusting me to partner with you to serve your children. You could do all this by yourself, yet to choose to include me in your plan.

INTRODUCTION

We all go through challenges, disappointments, and unfair situations. It's easy to let it overwhelm us to the point where we begin to despair and even think of giving up.

God would not have allowed it if you couldn't handle it. But as long as you're telling yourself it's too much, you'll find it impossible to overcome. You must develop a new perspective. You are strong in the Lord.

Anyone who has ever achieved anything meaningful in life has had to handle impossible situations boldly with courage and determination. You have to overcome all the odds to beat the challenges and develop your character.

When I look back of my journey, I have come to the conclusion that challenges are very instrumental in the shaping of our character and personality in pursuit of destiny. I was born in Nyalenda, a slum in Kisumu, the third largest City of Kenya which is along the shores of Lake Victoria.

I went through hundreds of challenges and could have been hopeless, but when you have focus and a positive attitude, you can change the impossible story to become a story of victory and a purpose full life. Never give up in life. Fight for yourself to become the person God intends you to be.

You've got to go through the worst times in life to get the best things in life. You've got to look at every challenge with a victor's mentality. Purpose that the adversity will not leave you bitter but better.

The fire of challenges will not consume you, but they will refine you into a pure and precious jewel. All the great people that we envy and quote had to suffer setbacks in their lives. My parents were poor and they could not afford to take me to better schools, but by the grace of God, when I was nine, I received a scholarship for education from Swedish Missionary Anna Lanson. She had worked with my father in the community water drilling project.

When Anna visited our humble home, I was assigned the duty of keeping her busy because I was a tiny girl, and there was no tangible work I could assist in taking care of our great guest.

I was told to talk to Anna as Mum prepared meals in the shack-like kitchen. I was little but bold. At the end of the visit, Anna asked my father what she could do for me. My father told her that I loved school, but he was facing a great challenge to educate me.

That was turning point of my life. Ann granted me a scholarship that gave me education, which was what I needed to rise above my miserable circumstances to realize my potential.

At times, the more bitter the lessons, the greater the successes. Even though the world is full of misery, it is also full of overcomers. You have to understand your challenges, face them, and subdue them.

In my next book, I will share testimonies of young people who had to overcome challenges and through the support of Maisha Project, their lives changed, and they now are productive members of the society.

I believe my life in the slum of Nyalenda and my educational journey were moments of preparation for the humanitarian work which I now do through Maisha Project. I am called by God to give hope for a better life to the most frustrated in the society.

My dream is to see widows and orphans live a better life, which was a catalyst for starting Maisha Project a program whose core mandate is to transform live and empower communities by providing lasting solutions to address poverty, hunger, disease and education.

As you read this book, I want to remind you that God created you with the potential to become whatever you desire, and every single thing that happens to you prepares you for greatness.

Every now and then, God will allow you to go through a rough path full of adversities. He is shaping you for what you will need to be effective as you connect to your destiny. You can even lose something valuable to you like a partner, family member, property, or business.

In the Bible, Joseph was sold by his brother to work as a slave. He lost everything he had, including his beautiful coat of many colors. He was betrayed by his brothers, thrown into a pit, sold into slavery, and spent years in a foreign prison for something that he didn't do.

But he didn't get dejected. He didn't start complaining. He stayed calm because he knew God would help him overcome. He kept his faith and remained focused on God. In the end, God used his predicaments to elevate him to become the prime minister of Egypt.

No person, no situation, no dissatisfaction, and no poverty can keep you from your destiny.

God not only gives us the best but the right things. You might think that a specific path is the best for you, but God knows the right path that will link you to your destiny. It might be a rough path full of adversities but later it will give you the stamina that you require to conquer your enemies like he has done for me through Maisha Project.

The greatest person on earth is the one who is able to conquer himself or herself—to conquer the obstacles, pain, hurts, scars, shame, loss, ans fear—and boldly face the future with zeal, passion, enthusiasm, and courage.

Overcoming all the impossibilities to conquer and win. Many times we are our worst enemy. If we could learn to conquer ourselves, then we will have a much easier time overcoming the obstacles along our path.

The future is too bright. But you have to stop hiding in your past shadows of low grades in school, molestation by close relatives, abortion, and drug abuse, and so on. We should not allow setbacks to disrupt our journey to our destiny. We need to remain focused, knowing that life is not always an easy path.

God will change your story if you are determined and prayerful to make your impossible situation possible.

Every day is a fresh opportunity to venture a new path and write a story. Each day is a new beginning to design new life.

If you do not fight for what you want now, you will fight against what you don't want later. Everything you have ever wanted is on the other side of fear. To gain anything substantial in life, you have to do something that requires you to go an extra mile. To win a marathon race, you have to undergo a vigorous training, stay disciplined and have a strategy. You have to change and set your mindset on your dreams and aspiration.

––––––

This book is designed to enable you discover your God-given potential and teach you how to harness them in order to make a positive contribution to yourself and the world. It also shows you how to turn your impossibilities into possibilities.

Be your best, do your best and be the best possible version of yourself.

——— —

"Life is full of beauty. Notice it. Notice the
bumble bee, the small child, and the smiling faces.
Smell the rain, and feel the wind. Live your life
to the fullest potential, and fight for your dreams."

—Ashley Smith.

EVERYONE HAS A PURPOSE

"There is no road to success but
through a clear, strong purpose."

—Thorton T. Munger

Nothing just happens. Everything takes place for a reason and a purpose. Sometimes, the delays, hiccups, struggles, setbacks, and stagnations are all set onto your path as a bridge that God uses to elevate you into the next level of influence he wants for you. As difficult as it can be, we should always set our minds and aspirations to positive outcome in the journey of life. Often, when we are determined to follow our own ways that make sense to us, God moves us to his path. In the moment, it looks so unpleasant, but later on it turns out to be the best path that aligns you to your purpose. You can look back and see this more clearly in retrospect.

God often protects his people by leading them into situations of temporary discomfort. These bring a greater dependence on him, and they strategically align us to our destiny and not in our own way and plan.

I was born in the slums of Nyalenda. When we think of slums, we often believe nothing good can come from there. Slums are filled with abject poverty, disease, crime, teen pregnancy, drug abuse, and more.

When I was nine, God connected me to Anna Lanson, a Swedish missionary who not only gave me the inspiration I dearly needed but also gave me a scholarship to pursue my education all the way to college. I had to take the opportunity that God brought on my path and rise above the slum's circumstances to realize my potential.

As I mentioned in the introduction, one of my favorite Bible stories is about when Joseph was put into slavery. His brothers sold him in order to ruin him and get him out of their lives, but they didn't know that they were connecting him to his destiny.

God had already prepared slave traders from a far country. He ordered them not only to pass near the pit but also to buy him for Potiphar's house. Joseph was so obedient to God, he also obeyed and respected his new master, which could not have been easy.

Eventually, God elevated him to become the prime minster of Egypt. God also orchestrated events—and worked on Joseph's heart—so that Joseph could forgive his brothers for what they had done to him. He could see the hand of God in all that had happened, and he was a part of rescuing his family from the famine they were going through.

Time and again, God will use our experiences in life as stepping stones to prepare us for what he has in store for us. The Scriptures tell us that he will even take the things the enemy tries to bring against us and turn them around to use them for our good.

I remember a friend of mine who was being sexually abused by her father and her shameless uncles. She hated herself and found refuge in church and a safe haven in school. She would run away from home because that was not a safe place for her.

May young girls across the world are going through abuse. They are living in fear and torment that ends up ruining their lives. I pray that God will change the hearts of those who plan and inflict evil in the lives of others. Justice must be rendered, and my hope is that we will see it.

God will always lead us into a journey of preparation, which at times takes a painful experience to make us transform our ways. God needs to shake us to wake us. Without such wake up calls, we will blindly fall onto the wrong path. We hate the evil, but we look for ways to God to turn it around and redeem it.

"It is in the small decisions you
and I make every day that create our destiny."

—Anthony Robbins

God wants us to surrender our will over to his. His love is there to motivate us and change us into the best path and plan, one much better than we could ever come up with.

I came from a fairly religious family. My father was a deacon in church, and my mother would pray for me and my siblings. When I joined high school, I rededicated my life to God. I became a leader of the Christian Union club. I loved it because school was a great place to escape from the challenges that the young people face in the slums.

Today, with the benefit of hindsight, I can only thank God for all of us. He orchestrated these events and circumstances to bring me to faith.

Sometimes it takes a painful experience to make us change our ways. That's why it is important to keep our eyes focused on him. We have to trust that when we are submitted to him—even if we don't understand—he is ordering our steps.

All things work together for our good. If you keep pressing forward, one day you'll look back and see how each setback played in God's master plan for your life. That's simply one part of the puzzle. There will be another piece that connects it all and gives it a significant and delightful outcome.

When I look at my ministry in Maisha Project, I can see the hands of God forming me to be able to help others to have a better and fulfilled lives by giving them the opportunities that many vulnerable children do not have especially in the developing countries of the world.

Here are important lessons I want to makes sure you know, understand, and live by:

Reconfigure your mindset.

One of the greatest assets that God has given us is our minds. You mind controls everything you do in life. It is therefore important to learn how to protect your mind from negative influences.

This is important because it will help you navigate your way through life, and God uses your level of mental growth to elevate you to a higher ground.

Romans 12:2 talks about a deep secret—if you want any transformation in your life, the easiest way to achieve that is to renew your mind. We read:

> And do not be conformed to this world, but be transformed by the renewing of your mind, that you may prove what is that good and acceptable and perfect will of God.

When I was younger, I did not know much about the importance of mind until I met my mentor Anna Lanson. She talked to me about the power of the mindset.

She told me that the quality of any picture depends on the focus of the photographer. It is through the purity of our mind that focus is created.

One of the greatest women in my life is Oprah Winfrey. I heard her for the first time on a television at a bus station on my way to visit my uncle in Nairobi. She spoke eloquently on many challenges young girls in in the world were going through. That was true in America, and I could relate to what she was saying on the other side of the world.

She was firm and courageous. I had never heard anyone speak so clearly on what she went through and how she overcame and achieved. From that brief encounter on television awaiting my bus, my mind was empowered to believe in the beauty of my dreams.

"It doesn't matter who you are, where you come from.
The ability to triumph begins with you. Always."

—Oprah Winfrey

The whole world knows about Oprah Winfrey, but let me share her amazing story. Oprah had to endure and overcome so much throughout her life to achieve her dreams. She received criticism about her weight and race, and she often was asked insensitive questions about her sexuality and capacity. However, that did not stop her. She kept doing what she loves most, and every day she grew became better.

As a little girl, she faced many challenges. Oprah was a victim of sexual abuse. She was repeatedly molested by her cousin, uncle, and a family friend. When she was fourteen, she became pregnant and gave birth to a child who died two weeks' later. Her resilience was evident at a young age when she went on to complete high school as an honors student, which earned her a full scholarship to college.

After college, Oprah worked hard in her career to move

from a local network anchor in Nashville to become a household name, international superstar, and the creator of so much of what we value and love.

That's my hero. She triggered something big in me.

When you look at her childhood, her personal triumphs are seen in an even more remarkable light.

> "The key to realizing a dream is to focus
> not on success but significance—and then
> even the small steps and little victories along your
> path will take on greater meaning."
>
> —Oprah Winfrey

Oprah Winfrey's Top 10 Rules for Success
Understand the next right move.
Seize your opportunity.
Everyone makes mistakes.
Work on yourself.
Run the race as hard as you can.
Believe.
We are all seeking the same thing.
Find your purpose.
Stay grounded.
Relax. It's going to be okay.

It would be wise to write these down and post them where you can see them every day to remember them. Perhaps start writing down what you think these rules for success might mean for you. How can you implement them?

Many people are going through deep challenges. I had to overcome many of them to remain focused on pursuing my dreams. It's my noble duty to guide others, and this is what inspired me to write this book. I want to encourage you that, despite the challenges in life, God has great plans for your life.

Zig Ziglar is one of the world's best-known sales trainers and motivational speakers. He has been recognized many times by United States' government, and he is extremely influential. I always quote him at my speaking engagements.

One of my favorites is:

"Success means doing the best we can with what we have. Success is in the doing, not in the getting; in the trying, not the triumph. It is a personal standard, reaching for the highest that is in us, becoming all that we can be." —Zig Ziglar

Achieving your purpose begins with a personal decision only you can make. It cannot be made by a group, though that might influence what you want in life. It's about you. It's about who you become and the values you express and embody.

One of the most important things in life is the types of questions you ask. The Scriptures clearly teach that if you seek, you will find. Deuteronomy 4:29 says: *"But from there you will seek the LORD your God, and you will find him, if you search after him with all your heart and with all your soul."* (RSV)

Finding is reserved for the searchers. Those who search find the best treasures. This is what I call the power of an entrepreneurial mindset.

I had to ask many questions to get connected with my purpose, and that gave me the desired results in terms of achievement. I want you to remember one thing—today is the best day to design your future, and anything you have achieved to date can be traced to the questions you have asked in your life.

When you have a positive mindset, it helps you to fight negative thoughts and to know the pressures you can handle and those you should let go. I have seen many young people in the slums succumb to drugs. I've watched girls get pregnant, which negatively impact their lives when they have to drop out of school. And I've seen incredible successes, which thrill me to no end.

Become emotionally intelligent.

Emotional intelligence is closely connected to mental health. It refers to the ability to recognize, perceive, and assess emotions in order to manage your behavior and how you act towards people and events in your life.

The devil uses your emotions to make you react to things the way he wants.

When you have control over your emotions, it protects you from walking away from what lies ahead. Your mind works hand-in-hand with your emotions. That is why it is important to scrutinize what gets into your minds because it has influence over your emotions.

When I look back on my growing up years in such a devastating circumstance in the slums, I can see how emotional intelligence was a key for me. It is essential for developing and equipping the young people and adults in terms of skills like communication and how life works and the realization of the God-given potential.

I have seen people who went to the same school as I did and who scored the same grades, but, even though they had the same opportunities to excel, some failed in life while others succeeded. Why? I think there was a disconnect between their dreams and attitudes.

Learn how your mind and emotions works. This understanding helps in establishing great relationships with others and aligning yourself with your purpose. Nothing is impossible if you are willing to try.

When you are good at managing your own emotions, and you can negotiate other people around you effectively, you become more thoughtful on how you behave, and it helps you avoid being judgmental about others.

God has endowed you with all the natural abilities you need to potentially have a brighter future and make the right choices. If you are going to succeed in life, you have to be in full control of your destiny and submit yourself to God's will as you walk in his path.

Monitor your thoughts.

We live in a world where you can easily slip down into bad groups or actions. There are so many things competing for your attention, and if you are not very careful on how you control your thoughts and emotions, you can go astray. I remember there were so many temptations in the slum of Nyalenda—alcohol, promiscuity, prostitution, drug abuse, and more.

You need to be alert so you can detect the challenges of life and overcome them, which includes being able to handle bad, ungodly company. You need to know what you stand for you and how to hold strong when temptations come. You have to resist just going with the flow and letting these destructive influences enter your life.

Recognize your feelings.

Research has shown that during a young person's transitional stages, he or she goes through many challenges—fear, irritation, and discontentment. The more informed you are about your emotional state, the more prepared you will be to control your reactions.

When you recognize your feelings properly, nothing will be impossible because you will have control over this important facet of your life. Instead of engaging in a confrontation, you can take the option of dialogue, peace-making, and reconciliation.

Be positive.

To succeed in life, you need to be positive in everything you do. This is the value of seeing and focusing on the good in any situation. It is knowing that things will come your way to pull you down. But when you are positive, you will know that any negative situation is just temporary. You have the power to overcome whatever you face.

This is what I always tell the young people under our support at Maisha Project. They are going to come across many challenges—feeling overwhelmed by emotions, broken relationships, family instigated challenges, and school-related ones like poor grades.

As you read this book, work on remaining positive about life. You will have far more control over any negative influences, and you will overcome fear to replace it with the hope that God puts in your heart. This gives you the fuel you need to succeed in life.

Fight negative influences.

Once you are born, you begin to fight negative influences, which the enemy will always use to derail you from focusing on your dreams. If you are going to be successful in this life, then you must be sensitive and alert in fighting against anything that is contrary that will pull you away from your anticipated life goals.

Wherever I travel—including here in Oklahoma where I live—I always look for positive vibration only. When you find yourself walking with negative and disgruntled people, you have to fight and break away from them.

The more you walk with them, the more they will influence your thoughts negatively.

David said that the one who walks in the counsel of God will be blessed. In Psalm 1, we read:

Blessed is the man who walks not in the counsel of the ungodly, nor stands in the path of sinners, nor sits in the seat of the scornful; But his delight is in the law of the LORD, and in His law he meditates day and night. He shall be like a tree Planted by the rivers of water, that brings forth its fruit in its season, whose leaf also shall not wither; And whatever he does shall prosper. The ungodly are not so, But are like the chaff which the wind drives away. (Ps. 1:1–4)

Find mentors.

The super achievers of this world have mentors. Mentors help you to navigate through the challenges of life. I take mentorship with uttermost importance because through this is how I was able to find my direction. I need this and benefit from it still, and it's why I help mentor young people and others. My life has changed as I've met and pursued mentors. It is why I am able to even write this book. Otherwise, right now I could be drinking cheap liquor and selling *omena* in Kisumu.

You can also get mentors from reading books. Some of my mentors lived in the past, and they still influence me as I read and meditate on their thoughts, trying to distill their lessons and apply them to my circumstances. You can find mentors from teachers, parents, classmates, and even friends who have noble character. If you want to succeed, then always surround yourself with people who are positive about life and are willing to invest in you for your good.

Improve your learning skills.

You have to develop an appetite for learning. The Bible talks about people perishing because of lack of knowledge. I learned this from my mentor and sponsor Anna Lanson, who was avid reader and a great teacher.

This lifestyle of learning did not happen for her out of the blue. She studied hard while in school, and afterwards, she started her missionary work in Sweden and traveled to other parts of the world like Africa. She is the one who made me see the better part of life, which gave birth to what I do today. I am forever grateful to her, even though she has passed on. It is my prayer that she continues to rest in eternal peace with Lord. I am positive that she is still learning!

You can develop learning skills by making the decision to listen to people to get value in what they say. Your aim should be always to treat every conversation as a learning opportunity. Be interested. Take notes. Ask questions. Press in to see what connections you can make.

Question the voices you listen to.

Over the years, I have learned to have a conversation with

myself. I have an internal dialogue where I try to lean into the truth about God, myself, and his world.

If your thoughts tell you that you are good for nothing, confront that lie by telling yourself what you are good at and how great you are before God. God loves you, and that matters! That's how faith works. It believes in what is not yet accomplished. You aren't finished. There is work to be done, and you are so valuable to God.

The reason why we have many young people going astray in the society today is because most of them do not know who they are. This makes them lose the grip of how to manage and control their lives. Some of the young people have allowed things like alcohol, illicit sex, drugs abuse, and bad company to control their lives. It's easy to do. It's tempting to give up and give in.

Practice self-control.

Any person who does not have self-control is a candidate for a disastrous life because your emotions and circumstances will control you in any way they want.

On the other hand, when you have self-control, you will be able to keep out of activities that can lead you astray.

For example, casual sex can lead to contracting sexually transmitted diseases or unwanted pregnancies that can cause school drop outs. All these can ruin your chances for a better life. Though it can turn out fine, I highly recommend you wait until you are in married.

The Bible teaches that sexuality is to be expressed in a

committed marriage relationship between a man and a woman. Though that may not be what you see around you, God's teaching is the way to go. Stay away from situations where you may be led astray or get in a place you cannot control. Talk to people about how to be wise with your body and emotions because this will greatly impact your future and your success. If you have strayed or erred, ask for forgiveness and chart a new path. Find a mentor to help you.

Be action oriented.

I did not just drop to the USA. I grabbed the opportunity that was available to many others. Action separates the successful from unsuccessful people. You have to take full responsibility of your life and design the future you want.

I am a woman who is from the land of some of the world's most famous athletes. Eliud Kipchoge is Kenyan's greatest world marathoner. He did not become a champion by chance. He took every opportunity to train and perfect his skills. He took action and overlooked the challenges from his humble background. But now, he is one of the richest athletes in the world, and many companies are seeking his endorsement for their products.

Think of who your heroes are, and study how they got to where they are today. Trace their action steps and hard work. Set out to emulate them as you go forward.

That is how Beatrice Williamson, a young girl from the slums of Nyalenda, now lives in one of the greatest countries in the world doing what she loves and supporting others.

I did not allow the slum to define me. I took action and overcame the limitation of where I grew up.

Nick Vujicic was born physically disabled without limbs. That seems impossible to overcome, doesn't it? Through believing in himself and working hard, he has become one of the greatest sources of inspiration and a world-famous motivational speaker. Look him up and learn from him.

Be compassionate.

Maisha Project is a mission born out of compassionate hearts of people in the world. The Bible says that when Jesus saw the people who were afflicted, he was full of compassion and reached out to them to help them because he loved them.

Many people are not compassionate. They only focus on what will benefit themselves. But when you are compassionate, you will understand people's needs and perspectives. As a result, you will have better non-judgmental relationships with others. This will reduce contention and conflict, which I believe is the cause of instability in the world.

When you are compassionate, you will exhibit great peace and enthusiasm, which will enable you to develop great relationships.

Be full of hope.

As children of God, we have hope that since he started a good work in us, he will be faithful to complete it (see Philippians 1:6). Hopeful people are optimistic, which makes them more creative. This helps them eliminate and overcome the obstacles along their paths.

Here is what Jeremiah 1:5 says in the Amplified version:

Before I formed you in the womb I knew [and] approved of you [as my chosen instrument] and before you were born I separated and set you apart, consecrating you [and] I appointed you as a prophet to the nations.

In this verse, God tells Jeremiah why he made him and his purpose for existence, which was to be sent as a prophet among the nations, He even tells Jeremiah that his appointment and ordination to the prophetic office happened way before he was born.

God has a purpose for you too.

Purpose precedes production, and it is the reason for production. Everything that has been made, whether visible or invisible, has a specific ordained purpose.

———

Be full of hope. Our life's purpose is part of God's story. God has shaped and prepared you to play a unique role in each step of your story. You have a destiny that will bring glory to God, share the grace of God, and extend the reign of God. Understanding your unique destiny starts with understanding what the Bible says about your purpose as one of God's children.

Growing up, we lived in a very tiny mud house. We had no running water or electricity. We could count the number of days we ate food, and school was not an option as my parents income was less than $1 a day. But God had positioned Anna Larson to come in my life and be a hand up to provide me with opportunity for education.

Something will happen for you. I don't know what it is. I hope this book might be a way for us to connect and that I could be an encouragement for you, even from far away. Keep at it. Don't give up.

Jeremiah 29:11 has been my anchor verse, and I give it to you: *"I know the plans I have for you,' declares the LORD, 'plans to give you hope and a future.'"*

God has been my hope, and he can be yours too.

PERSONAL RESPONSIBILITY

You must do the thing you think you cannot do.

—Eleanor Roosevelt

P ersonal responsibility is how you view yourself, the confidence you have to take charge of everything you are doing. If you have a high self-esteem, continue with that estimation of yourself (with humility) and don't let anything or anybody bring you down.

If you have been exposed to an environment of violence or always been put down, you will often feel you are not good enough. If you have a low self-esteem, spend time with people who value and appreciate you, who tell you positive things that encourage and build you up. On the other hand, spend very little time with people who bring you down and don't believe in you.

When I met Anna, the Swedish missionary, she believed in me and gave me her total support. Back when we didn't have a mobile phone, I would call through the landline telephone booth. I would wait for hours, but she would eventually call, and we would talk, and that encouraged me to keep working hard. We also exchanged letters that would take many weeks to arrive. I had to be patient, but I knew she would come through. I was so thankful for her support and encouragement. She invested so much care into me. She didn't have to do that. I will never forget, and I keep that in mind when I meet other young girls who need friends, supporters, and mentors.

It takes personal responsibility to avoid the people who always have something negative to say about you. Stay away from and ignore them.

Build your self-worth by listening to positive affirmations. God created you with enormous potential to achieve whatever dreams you want in life. Never underestimate yourself. Everything is possible for you if you believe.

Write down your own affirmations. Write: "I am beautiful. I am kind. I am successful. I am rich, and I am loveable." Put those on a 3x5 card and paste it where you'll see it every day. Stick it on your bathroom mirror, your computer if you have one, or your notebook—all over the place! Add to it as you find other things about yourself and what God about you. These are so important as you go through life.

Write down whichever kind words you would like to tell

yourself or whichever positive quality about yourself you would like to have. Make a list so your mind can process and internalize these affirmations for you to operate on them. Repeat positive affirmations about yourself before you go to sleep at night and when you wake up early in the morning. They should always be on the forefront of your mind.

We live in a world that is saturated by many negative influences that can be against you, but what you tell yourself will always be the most important words in your life. If you tell yourself positive things, you can live a happy life no matter what comes your way. If you tell yourself negative things, you will live a miserable life even if things are good. You'll be evaluating the world in a pessimistic way instead of an optimistic one. God wants us to look forward with hope and faith.

Think of this like a soundtrack that plays in the movie that is your life. What are the songs like that go on in the background? What are they about? Are they positive and hopeful or negative and depressing? If they aren't what you want, switch them out for something much better and more encouraging.

A good self-esteem comes from having a high value of yourself. It is the maturity that comes from how you handle it when someone talks negatively about you or something negative comes your way. You take it in, and you let it go. You put it in perspective because you know who you are. You know your strengths and weaknesses. You know you are infinitely loved by God and have a meaningful place in this world. You do not let other people bring you down or allow negativity to consume you. You know *whose* you are—you are a child of the most High God.

Know who you are.

Until you make peace with yourself, you will never be content with what you have as a person. How do you see yourself?

To deeply understand yourself, you must begin by answering the following question with a good sense of right and wrong:

- What are your values?
- What are your strengths and weaknesses?
- What challenges are you facing?
- What inspires and motivates you?
- What are you passionate about?
- What are your hopes and dreams?
- What are the failures you've already encountered?
- What gives you joy?
- What makes you frustrated and angry?
- Where do you find hope?

When you are honest with yourself, the truth shall set you free. Knowing yourself will help you identify the weaknesses that are within your ability to change and strengths that you can build upon to achieve your God-given potential.

When you understand your potential, it will motivate you to work hard on your goals because you know yourself. You have taken personal responsibility to accept who you are. You can restructure your life and become the best version of yourself.

In the same way, it's good to know what you aren't especially good at. We all have gifts and talents. Some are given by God and are innate. Others are developed. We can't all be good at everything, and we also cannot avoid all responsibilities we don't enjoy. We have to do hard work even in our weaknesses. But when we know what these are, we can get help, be humble, and mitigate against the worst possibilities. You also might see some of your weaknesses eventually turn to strengths as you get older and develop more.

What should you be aware of as a person?

You should be aware of your environment. Start to notice and catalog (at least in your mind) what the characteristics are of where you spend most of your time. This includes where you live, your family, and what you do each day. What is your place like and who are the people you interact with? This information will help you to be conscious of how this influences you as a person. As I lived in the slums of Nyalenda, I did my best to be aware of the state of affairs around me. I took notice of where I was and what people were doing.

You should do your own personal research about where you are. Work to understand your family dynamics, friendships, educational opportunities, town and city, and your friends. These are major influences in your life, and you should be thinking about how they are shaping you for good or ill.

When you are aware of where you are, you will know, approach, and overcome the challenges ahead of you in order to become the person whom God intended you to be.

God has created everyone with a different personality. Your personality influences your character and that helps others to know what your desires are. Your untapped potential will only manifest itself if you know who you are on the inside through your gifts and talents that you discover and develop. You should also understand the following:

- What are the common views that people have about you?
- Do you have any unpleasant experience, challenges, or struggles that you are reluctant to, afraid of, or ashamed to share?
- Do you have gifts or talents that are unknown to others?
- What do people say you do well?
- What are things that are more difficult for you?
- What are some of the highlights in what you've done thus far in your life?
- What are your regrets?
- What makes you angry, happy, or sad?
- What are the qualities and characteristics that you have learned about boys and girls, men and women, relationships, families, and marriage?

- What do you think about faith in God and your relationship with the church?

Enhance your self-awareness.

Identifying your gifts and strength can help you determine what you want to do with your God-given gifts. When you have a deep understanding of what God has put in you, nothing will be impossible to achieve. In Maisha Project, we help young people to grow in their gifts and talents because this has a potential of opening greater opportunities for everyone.

Be kind to yourself.

Never allow others to victimize you. Refuse to be brought down by any guilt within you which may be caused by failures.

You will experience plenty of misfortunes and shortcomings in your life. Forgive and encourage yourself. Learn from your past mistakes and move on but also accept the aspects of your life that you cannot change. If you have made mistakes, confess them to Christ, and he promises he will forgive you and cleanse you (see 1 John 1:9). You can move on. You are not trapped.

As I grew up, I knew my family did not have much in terms of wealth. Therefore, I had to work hard to get ahead. Your great contributions will not come without work. You have the power to overcome laziness, impatience, and other negative influences.

If you feel stuck, talk to a mentor, teacher, or counselor about what you are feeling.

Seek wise counsel.

The greatest secret to King David's success was the source of his wisdom. He walked with people who could give him good advice. He also relied on God, who protected and blessed him until his cup was overflowing.

The feedback from friends, family members, and your mentors can play an important role in enhancing your self-awareness. Trustworthy people around will always tell you the truth. When they see you are going astray, they will pull you back to the right path. Therefore, train yourself to deal with unpleasant feedback and to learn from constructive criticism. This will give you grounds for continuous improvement.

Self-reflect.

Deliberate reflections about your own feelings and behavior will enhance your self-awareness. Self-reflection also helps you discover your strengths which will encourage you to assume greater challenges and enable you to effectively deal with your weaknesses. Self-reflection will keep you from blindly following the crowd. It will ensure that you only engage in what suits and benefits you.

You might keep a regular journal to write down your thoughts. You might record your thoughts on your phone or computer. You should plan a time to do this—daily, weekly, monthly, quarterly, and yearly. You will learn from yourself as you write these reflections down and look back on what you are experiencing.

Expand your horizons.

Exposing yourself to the works of the most successful people in your area of gifting will open your mind to a world of infinite possibilities. It will broaden your view of life. This can be through reading books, getting wise counsel from mentors, or watching motivational and inspirational teachings. Expanding your horizon equips you with knowledge and skills to grow your gifting and talents.

When I came to Oklahoma, I was amazed by the many differences at the puzzle of life. I felt like I was in a completely different world. Even though I had planned and studied, I wasn't sure what to do or how to do it. Kenya and Oklahoma were completely different worlds. I had to learn how to navigate this new place so I could succeed.

———

I have been thinking of the story of the prodigal son, one I have always loved from childhood in Sunday school classes.

The prodigal son (we are not given his name) leaves his home, travels to a foreign country, and squanders his entire inheritance in riotous living. Unfortunately! He becomes broke and gets stranded. In his predicament, he begins to talk to himself.

In Luke 11: 17, we read that he came back to himself and decided to go back to his father: *"And when he came to himself, he said, How many hired servants of my father have bread enough and to spare, and I perish with hunger!"*

Despite the mess in his life, he changed his perspective, and God made a way for what seemed impossible. His father hugged him without any fear of the dirt on his clothes and ordered his elder brother to cover him with a robe.

Even though he had gone done the wrong path, he was able to correct his way and return home. This took courage, and he knew things might not turn out well. He had abandoned his family, home, and father. Nevertheless, he went back to his place, to his roots, and to his father.

He experienced tremendous favor from his loving, gracious father. He was more than accepted back. Think of what might have happened if he'd stayed in the pigsty instead of coming to his senses and returning home.

When you expand your horizon, you will think of things differently. You may end up changing your direction. You'll take important risks, and God will be with you to guide you as you move forward.

————

Personal responsibility is a critical component of human life. The world would undoubtedly be a better place if blame games stopped and individuals accepted responsibility for their actions. At times, people try to avoid personal responsibility, usually through blame-shifting.

I often think about how Adam tried to blame Eve for his sin Genesis 3:12. Cain tried to dodge responsibility Genesis 4:9. Pilate attempted to absolve his guilt in the matter of the crucifixion of Christ: *"I am innocent of this man's blood,' he said. 'It is your responsibility!"* (Matt. 27:24)

One of my favorite parables in the bible about responsibility is of the rich man who went on a journey. Before he left, he called his three servants. He gave one of them five bags of gold to take care of. This story exhibits the nature of different responsibility we have. God appreciated the effort put in. He didn't like it when the gold was buried in the dirt. He wanted to see effort put in, even if it took a risk.

Look for ways to take responsibility for what you have. Don't shirk it. Take pride in it.

GOD IS WORKING BEHIND THE SCENES

Many of life's failures are people who
did not realize how close they were
to success when they gave up.

—Thomas Edison

We all go through moments of anxiety, uncertainty, fear of the unknown, and challenges of life. It can feel like all of the forces of nature are working against us, and we're about to get knocked out. You may feel a deep sense of doom and death. You may have a clear and compelling vision that is flawless and sure. You know that if you achieve it, your life will instantly make a complete turnaround, and your success will be coming up quickly.

However, issues, situations, and disappointments seem to

be ganging up to thwart your dreams. God allows different scenarios to happen so you can learn vital lessons and acquire experiences that will be fundamental to achieving your visions effectively. He is working behind the scenes in your favor. He is crafting and welding things together with your best interests at heart. Sometimes, we feel like we are pressed against a rough, thick wall, and all hopes are gone.

But later, we see that God made a way the whole time. Why? Because he is in charge of every part of your life.

Every person—regardless of tribe, race, or gender—goes through tough situations in life. You won't be an exception. Those times are not pleasant, and they feel like they won't ever end. We all go through things in life that we don't understand. But did you know that God uses the dark spots in our lives as part of his divine plan? Do you know that God order our steps and destinies?

He knits experiences, divine connections, and provisions to make us be what he intended us to be and to move us to where he wants us to be.

Take a journey through the scriptures and see how people that did anything great went through dark places! I've already mentioned Joseph and the prodigal son. But also look at Moses, David, Ruth, Esther, Jonah, Paul, Peter, and Mary the mother of Jesus. None of them expected what happened to them. But they developed their potential in the valley they found themselves in.

Everyone has to go through situations that later give what is needed to achieve what God has planned. It's not all fun all the time. There are always rough patches.

The dark places are where you really grow. Think about what it's like inside a mother's womb where a body's organs and systems are knit together to make a human being that has five senses and functional organs. Consider how in order for a seed to germinate and grow, it has to be buried under the soil, "die," and later grow up to become a magnificent plant. You are a work in progress being prepared to shoot up. You may need to go through some darkness in order to get through to the new life planned ahead for you.

Think about how great athletes have to push themselves to the limits of exhaustion in order to prepare for the tests that are to come. They have to run sprints, lift weights, and go through anguish so they can be ready when the time comes.

Tough times prepare you for the greatness ahead so that other people will look up to you.

There are times when buildings have to be torn down in order to be remade for something better. There are difficult decisions to be made. It may feel like you're going backwards, but that may be necessary so you can get seeming even better built.

———

"Every great man, every successful man,
no matter what the field of endeavor, has
known the magic that lies in these words:
Every adversity has the seed of an equivalent
or greater benefit."

—W. Clement Stone

Recently, I was traveling back to my home city of Kisumu with a contingent of American medics. There were new beautiful roads all over in Nairobi and the Northern corridor. Buildings and developments had been built in what had previously been dirt and bushes. The construction meant that what I had been used to seeing had to be torn down and excavated. Though the squirrels and snakes were displaced, now we could host many children at Maisha Project, so we are so thankful for the work.

God uses your dark days to prepare you for what he has for you. Your character is tested and developed as you learn to trust, endure, and persevere. Your spiritual muscles grow stronger as you lean more on God (like running sprints for basketball or soccer). Just like any great project takes time and looks insignificant as you start, the end is always greater than the beginning.

When you are facing dark times like I did growing up—your challenges will be different, but you will have them—you have to discover your God-given potential to create your greatness so you can be a blessing to humanity.

Learn about the plan and purpose of the hard times. If the great people (like my secret mentor Oprah Winfrey) did not remain focused and resilience in the wake of tough heartbreaking challenges, they could not have become an inspiration to the world.

You may be going through a situation in life that makes you feel like God is so far away and unfair. Just know that the tough situation is not meant to finish you, but to give you a great experience and testimony. When David conquered Goliath, he had been prepared earlier when he had faced a bear and a lion. God had been getting him ready while he was growing up before he was the king. Everything in you is a work in progress. Just be focused and follow your God-given vision.

I had to go through many challenges before I eventually settled in Oklahoma. The slums of Nyalenda tried to pull me back, but with the help of God, I remained focused on my dreams and aspirations.

Today, I have the privilege to return home to Kenya every year to help change the lives of those back in my home town. It's amazing how God works.

Our God is one of abundance, and his intentions for you are to make you prosper and live a hopeful and fruitful victorious life. He is always working behind the scenes for your good.

———

"For I know the plans I have for you,"
declares the Lord, "plans to prosper
you and not to harm you, plans to give
you hope and a future."

—Jeremiah 29:11 (NIV)

Every person should have a desire to do something that will make someone else happy and feel appreciated. Unfortunately, most of us do not know how, when, or what to do, even with a lot of opportunities to serve others. Sometimes, God will prepare us for greatness by using unfamiliar paths so that we can acquire crucial skills and experiences that form the character you need for the tasks he wants you to perform in the future. He's getting you ready for what is to come. Don't forsake those learning opportunities!

I'm sharing some of lessons I have learned in my walk with God and in the development of my quest for changing lives. God prepared me in the wilderness through many hard experiences to have compassion and a sense of mission for others.

At a very early age in primary school, I always wanted to do good to people. There was a time I took my school sweater and gave it to a classmate who didn't have one. When I was asked the whereabouts of my clothes, I gave a "good lie" and said that it was lost. I would take my pocket money and buy sweets and give to the children around where we lived.

I wanted to be a doctor so I could save lives. I wanted to be a pastor to help preach to the less fortunate who didn't know Jesus.

I was brought up in a very humble, poor family. We often went to school without food, and we wore torn clothes that didn't fully cover our bodies. My parents could not afford a needle and thread to stitch out our dresses.

What did that do to you Aunty Bea?

It gave me an understanding of what it means to go to school barefoot from Monday to Friday. I knew I could attend church without decent clothing. My first decent shoes were the plastic ones known as sandaks. The hot sun of Kisumu could heat the sandak and cause burns and blisters on my toes, but that did not bother me because I had something on my feet. It was better than going barefoot!

I know what it means to sleep hungry. We often had to save the little flour available to prepare a little porridge for the children.

———

"The difficulties and struggles of today
are but the price we must pay for the
accomplishments and victories of tomorrow."

—William Boetcker

The challenges of poverty can extremely affect the self esteem and academic performance of children. But even still, even in the midst of awful circumstances, I know nothing is impossible if you don't underestimate yourself.

Upon completion of my primary school education, I was able to join Aluor Girls High School, one of the best schools at the time due to my exemplary performance. I loved the school so much because it took me from the challenges of the slum of Nyalenda to a more secure and peaceful environment.

My parents didn't have the money to take me through high school, but God sent Anna Lanson, and she took care of all the expenses needed for all the time I was in school.

A few years ago, when we hosted the Maisha and Cultural Camps for our students, I was moved by a boy who remained behind after everybody else had left the camp meeting. He helped collect the scattered bottles of soda.

He caught my eye for two reasons. First, he started to collect the bottles of soda and putting them in crate without being told to do so. The second reason is because he was consistent in helping out to do chores voluntarily. I wanted to have a chat with him and find out more. Days later, he did not come back to our functions, but he kept on popping into my mind.

One afternoon, on our way to Kisumu from the village, I spotted him walking along the road, and I asked the driver to stop so I could talk to him. I was heartbroken that he was a street boy, but I was also moved by his acts of compassion and service. I asked him to him to return to the camp, and he did. From this encounter, we enrolled him in a nearby school called Omungi Primary School in class six. We gave back to him like what had been given to me.

Today, he is a graduate student from Maseno University with a degree in Psychology, and he is an inspiration to the children at Maisha Project and also to his neighborhood. Nothing is impossible if you believe in the beauty of your dreams.

If I did not remember my journey and the hands of compassion from the people who came to help me, this boy might be doing drugs, robbing and pickpocketing people, or even rotting in jail or dead.

————

"Many of life's failures are people
who did not realize how close they
were to success when they gave up."

—Thomas Edison

God let me face challenges to learn the value of humanity and service. His providential hand led me to become a community leader helping those who were dispersed in the world and ended up in Oklahoma City. I worked at a church as a pastor, and that helped me develope passion, experience, and exposure to help others.

I have been a work in progress, and God has been the chief master planner connecting the dots behind the scenes. As per Psalm 23, he was anointing my head and setting a table for me before my enemies.

Our God is an extraordinary master, even when we think our lives have reached a dead end just like Joseph must have felt when he was thrown in the pit and then put in prison.

God provides enough grace and makes everything possible for you and me.

He is crafting everything to work together for our good and to serve his purpose. Do not be afraid when you see that your life isn't where you want it to be yet. Joseph could have felt the same when he was thrown into a pit and prison, but he was focused on his dreams. He exercised diligence wherever he was assigned. There was sufficient grace in all the circumstances he found himself in, and the hand of God was with him. He was work in progress. God was preparing him for the big tasks ahead.

God doesn't provide barely enough. He provides *more than enough* in every area of our lives. There is no such thing as wasted time to God. He uses an experience of ordinary people to do extraordinary things in the lives of others, and he will use you. Sometimes we may ask God for success, and he gives us physical and mental stamina. We might pray for prosperity, and we receive an enlarged perspective and increased patience leading to growth.

"To be successful, the first thing
to do is fall in love with your work."

—Sister Mary Lauretta

God does not waste an experience. He allowed me to go through the challenges in my life to prepare me for the task ahead of empowering people to transform their communities. He was preparing me to write this book to empower people to transform for you to read and be inspired.

Realizing where I belong and who holds my life inspired

me to get motivation from God and from the bible verses which have been inspiring me day by day.

Here are some of them:

- *When you pass through the waters, I will be with you; and when you pass through the rivers, they will not sweep over you. When you walk through the fire, you will not be burned; the flames will not set you ablaze.* — Isaiah 43:2
- *And we know that all things work together for good to them that love God, to them who are the called according to his purpose.* —Romans 8:28
- *So do not fear, for I am with you; do not be dismayed, for I am your God. I will strengthen you and help you; I will uphold you with my righteous right hand.* —Isaiah 41:10
- *Be strong and courageous. Do not be afraid or terrified because of them, for the LORD your God goes with you; he will never leave you nor forsake you.* — Deuteronomy 31:6

May the Lord use your past and current situations to impact and change lives. He doesn't waste an experience, but you have to totally surrender unto him. He loves you too much to allow you go through that experience without anything good for you. He is working behind the scene, behind that loss, behind that trial, behind that tragedy—and the end result will be glorious.

The lessons you learn from going through a difficult situation will help you to move to the next level achievement. Overcoming an obstacle is the gateway to your greatness. You will look back and say something like I do: "I thank God for having allowed me to go through the experience of the slums of Nyalenda because it opened a way for me to the purpose full life I live today."

God has an appointed time to fulfill the visions, dreams, and desires in your heart. Just because it has taken a long time or it failed up to this point doesn't mean that it's not going to happen. Don't give up on those dreams. Don't be complacent about pursuing what God has placed in your heart. Don't give up on God because he will never give up on you.

God is a faithful, therefore, no matter how long it takes or how impossible things looks. If you'll stay faithful in your work, you will succeed.

God will use your enemies as your stepping stone. The condition that seems to push you down will be the bridge to your major breakthrough.

The enemy will come into your thoughts to discourage you. But don't let him. Keep going and trusting God. He's going to bring some sort of Goliath in your life so you can defeat him. That's a step for you on your way to being a king or queen.

Don't be frightened. Our courage and faith grow in tough times. When the enemy puts you under pressure, God prepares you to overcome more than you think you can. The Lord will use all of these difficult situations to push you ahead, and those around you will be able to watch how you handle it.

God will use your enemy to push you forward. Soon enough, you will say it was good that it happened. David said, *"It is good Goliath came that I was promoted from a shepherd to a King and given the King's daughter to be my wife."*

God created you to be successful before you were born, He has a plan for your life, and he knows everything that will come your way. These moments are not ordinary. They are destiny-changing ones that are designed to make us great.

The book of Ecclesiastes states that time and chance come to every person. This means you will have opportunities to meet the right people, advance your career, and fulfill your dreams. You will have chances to give and be a blessing to others like we do in Maisha Project. We always thank God —over one thousand orphans and widows have seen their lives be transformed for good.

God will also give you the wisdom to seize opportunities to lay a foundation for your destiny and for others. God has already prearranged ways that your blessings will come to you. Things might not look good right now, but your seasons of favor and increase are already marked by God for your future. Don't miss these moments by giving up. Don't get distracted by your current circumstances.

You are much more than what you are going through in your life right now. Get rid of any distractions that are threatening you from doing the will of God.

The bible states that we become what we think about. When you think thoughts of success, victory, joy, and peace —your life will be filled with success, victory, joy, and peace.

You should not be worried about what is going on around you. Just work hard and your success will be guaranteed.

My friend, set your mind on victory and move forward to claim it. Change your mindset and dream big. The challenges you are facing are temporary. The supernatural God will direct your steps and lead you to your appointed time for breakthrough. He is working behind the scenes on your case.

Make a decision to change how you see the obstacles and the circumstances that bring you pain and heartbreak. Raise your faith, and know that all your past failures and frustrations are actually foundation stones to greatness.

That is the story that will be written into a bestseller book when you look back on this situation you're in now. Step up!

Isaiah teaches us, *"As the heavens are higher than the earth, so are my ways higher than your ways and my thoughts than your thoughts"* (Is. 55:9 NIV).

God's dreams for your life are so much bigger than you can imagine. He wants to bless you and enlarge your territory. Don't allow the circumstances of life to dilute your thoughts. Choose God's thoughts by meditating on his word because his ways and thoughts are far higher than ours.

The Scripture states that we should remain focused. We read that we are to *"set your mind on things above."* Those "things above" are God's thoughts and his ways. Having higher thoughts means thinking:

"I am blessed and highly favored. I am holy. I am more than a conqueror. I am the best there is. I am above only and not beneath. I am the head and not the tail. I am a victor, not a victim. I am righteous, and my path shines brighter and brighter to the full day!"

When you allow God to guide your thoughts, he will direct your steps to become an overcomer living a life of abundance.

Here is another verse that you should know well:

And the Lord answered me, "Write the vision; make it plain on tablets, so he may run who reads it. For still the vision awaits its appointed time; it hastens to the end, it will not lie. If it seems slow, wait for it; it will surely come; it will not delay." (Hab. 2:2)

———

God allowed the lion and the bear to attack the sheep so that David would fight back and gain the courage and the skills to fight and win against Goliath. God was preparing him.

What I went through in Nyalenda was equipping me for the challenges ahead. God is also putting the right people along your path to help you carry the vision he has for in your life. He will give you the right experiences, exposure, and the right attitude to help you achieve your dreams.

Arise and shine, for it's your time to go an extra mile beyond your current limit, and enjoy the great overflow and outcomes that will come your way. I declare a great breakthrough, favor, divine idea, divine strategy, divine connection, divine provision, and a new song in Jesus' name.

It is God who put every dream and promise that is in your heart, and his aim is to bring it to pass. So hold on to that vision today and declare, "My time is coming. God is working behind the scenes on my behalf. I will fulfill my destiny!"

When you believe and speak to your dreams, it will begin to take shape and manifest into reality. This will increase your faith and strengthen you as you walk to the city of success.

Are you going through a hard time? Maybe you recently lost a loved one or your job. Whatever you're dealing with, I want you to know that you're not alone. Something good is coming from the tough spot you're in right now.

Jesus experienced hard times too, and he endured to the end. All things work together for our good. When something doesn't happen the way we would like it to happen, we can believe God will work things out for good.

———

"I've always tried to go one step past wherever people expected me to end up."

—Beverly Sills

I have seen many young people across the world face trials in life that even pushed them to suicidal thoughts due to some self- inflicted mistakes. I know God can change that to your good. Don't give up. If you feel these thoughts, talk to someone about them. The world needs you!

Everyone goes through seasons of challenges in life. One of the enemy's traps is to isolate and discourage you. If you're going through a tough season as you read this book, I want to encourage you to have a positive attitude of expectancy.

You are more than a conqueror, and God will give you strength to stand during difficult times. Nothing is impossible if you believe and take action to change it.

It might be today, next week, next month, or next year, but you will see that God is faithful. Through faith and patience, you will get to your destiny and increase in wisdom and strength.

My friend, your appointed time is coming. God is working behind the scene in your favor. God is going to change your ashes for beauty.

Maybe you are in the valley of disappointment and loneliness, but that is not your final destination. Divine connection and provision is coming your way. You may be going through a tough time like Joseph in the pit. You may not understand it, but God allowed this to come to pass so you can walk step by step out it.

You are destined to win. You will succeed in this life. There will be roadblocks and obstacles, but everything is possible, and you are going to succeed in everything you do. So don't underestimate yourself. Keep pressing forward and your dream will come true. Everything takes time, so be patient while you learn from life.

Don't just sit there thinking about the magnitude of the problem—no! Stand firm and walk towards the problem. Each day, do something that move in the direction of your goals. Our consistency in our actions must be in positive harmony with our thoughts.

We must believe that achieving our dreams is possible, and we have what it takes to make them work in our favor. We have to write each goal and take personal responsibility to achieve them all in due time with hard work and perseverance. You have this promise—regardless of the fire, mountains, and valleys, you will still be standing because you are a child of the highest God.

Isaiah teaches us another important truth:

I am the LORD. That is my name, and I will not give my glory to another or my praise to idols. See, the former things have taken place, and I'm announcing the new things before they spring into being I'm telling you about them. (Is. 42:8-9)

We often get discouraged and feel like giving up because things don't turn out the way we anticipated. It is important that we look at the big picture and not let these temporary setbacks make us lose focus of where we are going.

Behind the scenes, God is putting together the right ingredients to bake the best cake for your life. God expects you to fully and wholly trust in him to make your life glorious.

———

"I would rather attempt something great
and fail than attempt to do nothing and succeed."

—Robert Schuller

Finally, I want to remind you that you can trust God because he is fully aware of what he is doing and knows what is best for you. While God is at work in your life behind the scenes, it is critical that you place your complete trust in him and his mighty power to make a way where there seems to be none.

BOUNDARIES & LIMITS

"Believe in yourself and you will
turn more of yourself into practical use."

—Anonymous

We stand in the wake of Abraham Lincoln, the great American who signed the Emancipation Proclamation. This momentous decree came as a great beacon light of hope to millions of Negro slaves who had been seared in the flames of withering injustice. It came as a joyous daybreak to end the long night of captivity.

And we live after Martin Luther King, Jr., who stood at the nation's capital and reminded us that we still have a dream despite the difficulties and frustrations of the moment we are in. Remember these words:

I have a dream that one day this nation will rise up and live out the true meaning of creed…. I have a dream that my four little children will one day live in a nation where they will not be judge by the color of their skin but by the content of their character.

—Martin Luther King, Jr

Today, as we recall this great speech, we remember the dreams Dr. King had for America despite the sufferings encountered by the African-Americans at the time.

As I write this book, what was once a dream, thought, idea, and a vision has come much more realized. I've had to work to see this small project accomplished, and it's been no easy task!

MLK had a much bigger dream, one that is far more complicated to achieve. What would he think if he were alive today? Would he be thrilled at how much farther we've come than where we were then?

His children are now free, just the way he wanted. He wanted people to have boundaries with each other. He wanted respect for each other.

A part of any dream is figuring out what gets in its way or what keeps it from being accomplished. We have to put barriers and boundaries around whatever is seeking to destroy or imperil our dreams. Some of those might involve time and money. If you want to pay for training, you may need to forego a new car. That would be a boundary you've placed so you can achieve what you wish. Or you may have to put away games on your phone if they suck up valuable time that you need to move forward for your accomplishments.

Boundaries are what you can and cannot accept from someone else. If you know yourself well, you will have limits that people can not infringe on. You will not accept it when people treat you with disrespect. If someone belittles you, you will stand up for yourself. If someone tells you to do something you are uncomfortable with, you will say NO. You have to say no to what you do not want to get into your space. You say no because you believe in something right. If someone is not good for your space, keep away.

Work on your attitude.

Your attitude determines the state of the world you live in. It is the foundation for every success and every failure you have had and will have. Your attitude will make you or break all your limits. Attitude can be defined as emotional readiness to express favor or lack of favor towards something. It can also be defined as beliefs, feelings, and values that cause us to act in a particular way.

A positive attitude refers to the ability to be optimistic about life, people, and circumstances even when conditions are unfavorable. It is the power to overcome challenges.

Your attitude determines your achievements in life because it directly affects your actions. People must develop a positive attitude in order to deal with the challenges of life.

I can assure you that you are going to find yourself in many unfavorable conditions that are beyond your control.

When I was in Nyalenda slum, there was nothing much I could do to change that, but every day I remained positive and prayed that God would change my life.

In spite of your circumstances, which you cannot fully control, you can choose to maintain a positive attitude for the sake of your dreams. Your attitude is communicated both verbally and non-verbally, and the people you interact with can detect it.

The value system we uphold is also an indicator of our attitude towards life and all the boundaries around life. You may have interacted with people who exhibit a protective nature about everything. This is because a negative attitude causes them to constantly point out the issues in everything and focus on the flaws and problems in themselves, other people, and the world around them.

A good attitude creates boundaries for the power to put in the effort required to achieve our goals. This then creates the momentum for our progress. On the other hand, a bad attitude creates boundaries around us that prevent us from moving forward to achieve success.

A negative attitude is caused by low self-esteem, unresolved conflicts, fear, uncertainty, stress, anger, a lack of faith, and anxiety.

Changing your attitude is a personal choice that requires you evaluate the connections between your behavior and your circumstances. This helps you deal with any underlying causes through determination and discipline. You can work to eliminate negative vibrations from your life.

Your attitude today is an important part of creating your

future. Therefore, commit to developing a positive attitude and boundaries to protect you.

Love and protect yourself.

People can also be their worst enemies because they don't believe in themselves. Break the boundaries of hate you have for yourself. Sometimes people won't believe in you, but brush that off immediately.

You have to accept yourself. We all have strengths and God-given potential which we should celebrate while we work on improving our weaknesses. However, there are things we cannot change about ourselves—our height, skin color, gender, and so on. The only thing we can do is to create a powerful block to protect us. We need to accept love and be kind to ourselves.

Talk about what you need.

Do not expect other people to read your mind. You must create learn to express your needs in a manner that is respectful to everyone who gets within your boundaries. Speaking up for yourself is a key skill in moving forward.

This will be important in your career, jobs, dating, marriage, and just about anything. Remember that when you talk about what you need, you do so with dignity and respect. You may not even get what you want, but it's important to know what to ask for and be able to deal with the consequences. Of course, you need to know what you need, and that can be tricky to figure out at times.

Reflect on everything.

When you are overwhelmed by issues and the challenges of life, it's good to sit down and reflect on what you can do. That reflective time you have with yourself will help you create positive boundaries and protect your wellbeing and close out negative vibrations. Reflect on your needs and your life every now and then to determine what is good for you as a person.

This is a good time to get a journal going if you don't have one. You can buy a physical blank book, or start with pieces of paper, or begin a new file on a computer or your phone. Take notes about what you're thinking and feeling. Write down what makes you happy and sad, angry and joyful, want to run away or move towards.

If you keep this up, you will know yourself well over time.

Assist others.

Assisting others is one of the most powerful things a person can do. This can be done through affordable material gifts or by giving a service. In my non-profit organization, I have learned many values and skills from assisting others. When you assist others, you break all types of boundaries like fear and doubt. This gives you a positive outlook about what can and will come your way.

I would encourage every person to find an organization and volunteer to give a service. This will help you to develop leadership skills and become useful to the community. You should also serve others at home, in your church, and in your neighborhood.

Listen to yourself.

We are all going to encounter issues that are overwhelming and make us feel helpless. When you are in that situation, it can be very challenging and disturb your peace.

This can lead to low self-esteem and depression, which are causes of drug abuse, suicide, and other self-destructive behaviors.

Depending on what is happening in your life, your internal dialogue can enhance negative feelings in you or foster positive feelings. You have to learn to put boundaries on negative issues that threaten to overwhelm you.

Take stock of where those negative thought come from. Can you trace them back to when they started or how they grew? Are they attached to a certain place or person or event? As you get to know yourself, you'll dig deep into some of what comes up in your thoughts and feelings.

Work on these. Identify what is true and what isn't. Some of what you think and feel are not accurate. Change these negative vibrations by putting a boundary around them, that at least you will evaluate them to see if they are true or not.

Negative internal dialogue is the type of thinking that puts you down. Learn to encourage yourself by talking to and believing in yourself. This leads to a positive attitude which creates the momentum for success.

Carefully choose the people you walk with.

Your friends are a reflection of your attitude. Your character is closely in line with the people you surround yourself with. Therefore, choose friends with high self-esteem, a cheerful spirit, and positive energy because their positivity will be contagious.

Look at your friend group and see if it best expresses the type of person you are or want to be. There are a ton of stories and movies about people in groups or cliques who later realize they had it all wrong. Be careful not to miss out on what others have to offer. Be friends with many different types of people that challenge and encourage you.

Protect your vision.

Vision is seeing your future from where you are standing now. You look ahead to picture what is before you.

If you don't have boundaries around yourself, you will lose your vision. You have to protect your mind with the things you want to achieve in life by engaging in positive thoughts, talk, and behavior. This is because your mind is strong and will direct your effort towards what you want to achieve, and this will depend on how you protect your vision.

Don't dwell in the past—instead, focus on the future. Reflect on the past and learn from it, but move forward with what you discover. Make it positive.

People may push you to participate in the negative things that they engage in. When these propositions happen, put a boundary around the negative experiences by forgiving and moving on. Failure to do so will cause you to develop bitterness that will be manifested by having a negative attitude towards your offenders. Don't dwell in the past. Focus on the future.

Develop an appetite for reading.

The secret to maintaining a positive attitude is to enrich your mindset. You have to do that as a matter of urgency. You may have seen people who develop a negative attitude towards learning which leads them to focus on failures. There are many self-help books that are intended to help people address various challenges in life. Get those and read them. Read as many as you can get your hands on. When you find one you love, reread it many time.

You can also read the life stories of other like Mother Teresa, Nelson Mandela, and Dr. Martin Luther King. Biographies will give you the inspiration you need through the changes they brought to the world and what they had to do to get to where they needed to be.

Set a goal of reading ten minutes a day, and then see if

you can get through one book a month. Think of how many books you could get through over ten years if you read one or two books a month instead of wasting time in other areas.

Read in your interest areas, but also be willing to take suggestions and expand your horizons. Ask others for their recommendations.

Be physically active.

Physical activities help bodies to charge and get refreshed. I do a lot of charity walks to fundraise for the needy to get food, shelter, and medicine. It is also a way of keeping fit and healthy at the same time.

When you participate in physical activity, it helps you fight stress and stave off any self-sabotaging behavior that will affect your joy, relationships, and general wellbeing. Physical activities are important in creating boundaries against anything that is causing any negativity.

Find physical activities you love to do, but include more than sports. Consider gardening or hiking. Also think about taking dancing classes, or learning how to canoe or kayak. You might broaden your horizons by trying acting classes or pottery. Get out and move your body and your brain, and this is a good way to meet interesting people.

———

This is where I back up and write to you that you cannot do absolutely everything. At least not yet!

You can't yet swim the English Channel, though people have.

You can't yet go to the moon, though people have.

You may have physical or situational limitations that seem insurmountable. As you work through these and process them, keep on asking God what he wants for you. Some of the impossible things may happen. But don't rush God either. Don't get married to the wrong person because you want to and can't wait. Don't buy things you can't pay for. Don't keep on with unhealthy living.

God can do tremendous things through you, and we need that in our world. Realize that he's doing other things through other people, and rejoice in that as well.

DARE NOT QUIT

"Moderation is the keynote
of lasting enjoyment."

—Ballou

I want to encourage you if you want to quit or are feeling as if God no longer thinks about you. Our God loves you so much that he has engraved your name on his palm. The prophet Isaiah wrote, *"I have engraved you on the palms of my hands; your walls are ever before me"* (Is. 49:16). You may be experiencing a chain of failures and consistent disappointments. Sometimes when you are almost at the finish line, you experience a puncture, and success turns instantly into failure.

Stick to the fight when you're hardest hit—it's when things seem worst that you mustn't quit!

Forget the bad and disappointing things that have

happened in the past. God is doing a new thing. Isaiah writes, *"I am doing a new thing! Now it springs up; do you not perceive it? I am making a way in the wilderness and streams in the wasteland"* (Is. 43:19).

When life becomes hard, do not quit! When you get frustrated, do not quit! When you want to quit—DO NOT QUIT!

In my life, I have gone through fire, brimstone, and the ugly storms of life. I have gone for days without food. I have tasted poverty, shame, disgrace, and disappointment. This book is about courage, faith, and hope.

I went through what seemed like endless amounts of frustration and struggle, and the most important thing I had to do was tell myself "Do not quit!"

> "On the path of self-realization, there are only
> two mistakes a seeker can make. One: Not
> treading the path at all and two: not going all the way."

> —Om Swami

Living the life I'm talking about takes discipline. When you are disciplined as a young person, your chances of success go up significantly. I'll bet you didn't like it or appreciate it at the time, but it's good for. That was true then, and it's true still now even though it looks different.

It is not possible to be persistent without being patient. Patience feeds persistence, and it boosts your determination. Patience is reminding yourself that you must continue without complaining until you are fully satisfied with the outcome.

Whenever you feel like quitting, ask yourself questions. The mind has a unique ability to mold itself.

If you say, "I can't do it," your mind shuts down, and your body follows suit. When you ask "How can I do it?" it gets your mind into action, and it comes up with answers so you can discover a solution.

My questions were always, "How do I shift to start my own ventures, and how will I survive?"

Going a step at a time made it easier to persist, and it's one of the best decisions at I ever made. I kept going and going and going.

Today, Maisha Project is changing lives in Africa. We are empowering people to transform their communities, and that is so satisfying. I'm glad I didn't quit!

I have always wanted to write this book, but I kept on procrastinating. I wasn't sure I could do it (I have doubts I have to work through too). When I met Wycliffe, he inspired me to begin the book and follow through. Now am an author and a motivational and entrepreneurship speaker. I had to quit making excuses.

Setting small goals to attain bigger ones is a secret that many do not know. It is easier to train your mind by vowing to do something for a shorter period so it may allow you to honor bigger commitments.

For example, you are far more likely to keep your vow if you resolve to not smoke for the next one day as opposed to never smoking for the rest of your life. Each time you stick to your word, you gain inner strength, and you get a step closer to taming your mind.

If you want to run a mile, you start with going down the driveway and back. Add to it, and your distance will get longer. Don't worry about the full thing at the beginning.

Subsequently, executing bigger plans and attaining larger goals becomes easier. Divide them into smaller steps and watch them multiply.

To experience the joy, go right till the end. Whatever it is that you do, do not quit till you are satisfied and done. Keep going one step at a time. Keep crossing one hurdle at a time. Just like traveling at night, you only see several meters in front of you with the headlights on, but that is enough to travel a journey of several thousand miles. Similarly, each step takes you closer towards your destination.

If you fear God and trust him, he will fulfill your heart desires. In Proverbs we read, *"What the wicked dread will overtake them; what the righteous desire will be granted"* (Prov. 10:24).

If your ways are right with God, he will always do anything that is good for you regardless of how impossible it might look at the beginning. Sometimes, when you begin to analyze the things taking place in your environment (like it was for me in the slums of Nyalenda), you can be discouraged and feel like God is far away and doesn't care. God's intention for you is that you prosper. Your part is to walk with God, obey his commands, work hard, and remain focused on your dreams and vision. He will fulfill them.

In Jeremiah we read the prophet say, *"I will find joy doing good for them and will faithfully and wholeheartedly replant them in this land"* (Jer. 32:41)

Is this you? Have you ever questioned your own existence because the potential of your dream no longer excited you but haunted you? God puts dreams in us and expects us to trust him to fulfill that dream. He does this for his glory.

People who encourage you to quit or ridicule you for pursuing a dream are living in a bitter state. They probably quit something important, and now they want to contaminate others. Don't listen to the negative talk from the pessimists. They don't hold your destiny, and they are just distracters.

Quitting is a mental state that overwhelms us. To prevent this, continue to keep your mind focused on the end result.

> "The man who moved a mountain was the one
> who began carrying away small stones."
>
> —Chinese Proverb

When your mind is filled with images of results, it will become so real that it's impossible to separate yourself from it. It is important to finish what you started. You were given a dream. Don't abandon it but pursue it until manifestation occurs. You are closer than you think. Keep going. You will make it. Stay encouraged, motivated, and have your best day yet.

Nothing can stop this lady Beatrice from reaching her dreams.

Real Winners Don't Give Up!

Never ever give up, my friend! Keep on keeping on until you become the best of what you were meant to be.

Keep these verses in mind:

"You will not have to fight this battle. Take up your positions; stand firm and see the deliverance the LORD will give you... Do not be afraid; do not be discouraged. Go out to face them tomorrow, and the LORD will be with you." (2 Chron. 20:17)

"Be strong and courageous. Do not be afraid or terrified because of them, for the LORD your God goes with you; he will never leave you nor forsake you." (Deut. 31:6)

My advice to you is—just don't quit! Keep on going.

Even when it looks like nothing is ever going to work for you, DO NOT QUIT!

Abraham Lincoln never quit. Born into poverty, Lincoln was faced with defeat throughout his life. He lost eight elections, twice failed in business, and suffered a nervous breakdown.

He could have quit many times but he didn't. Because he didn't quit, he became one of the greatest presidents in US history.

Here is a sketch of Lincoln's road to the White House:

- **1816** His family was forced out of their home. He had to work to support them.
- **1818** His mother died.

- **1831** Failed in business.
- **1832** Ran for state legislature—lost.
- **1832** He lost his job and wanted to go to law school but couldn't get in
- **1833** Borrowed some money from a friend to begin a business and by the end of the year he was bankrupt. He spent the next seventeen years of his life paying off this debt.
- **1834** Ran for state legislature again—won.
- **1835** Was engaged to be married, fiancé died, and his heart was broken.
- **1836** Had a total nervous breakdown and was in bed for6 months.
- **1838** Sought to become speaker of the state legislature—defeated.
- **1840** Sought to become elector—defeated.
- **1843** Ran for Congress—lost.
- **1846** Ran for Congress again—this time he won. Went to Washington and did a good job.
- **1848** Ran for re-election to Congress—lost.
- **1849** Sought the job of land officer in his home state—rejected.
- **1854** Ran for Senate of the United States—lost.
- 1856 Sought the Vice-Presidential nomination at his party's national convention—received fewer than one hundred votes.
- **1858** Ran for US Senate again—again he lost.
- **1860** Elected president of the United States.

You must hold on and keep moving, keep pressing and keep rowing. I promise you that you will achieve your dreams and aspirations.

Don't drop your guard. Keep focused.

"Moderation is the keynote of lasting enjoyment."

—Ballou.

We all differ in how we have fun, but the most important part is having self-control. It is important to be responsible as you perform your daily routines. You should not expect that people will always be there to police you.

When I was growing in the slum of Nyalenda, I saw many young people drop their guard of responsibility to indulge in ways that were self-destructive.

I don't expect that you will be 100 percent perfect. All am praying for is that in everything you do, you will practice moderation. This creates a balance in life. You have to prepare for the future. If you get too loose in your life, you will lose track of where you want to go. You also need guidance to give you the tools that will help you navigate through the challenges of life.

Before you do something, ask yourself whether your idea of fun will make you regret the next day or if it will make you have moments or experiences to remember. Your friends can make you have memorable moments, but others can lead you to moments where you are under the influence of alcohol and drugs. This can lead to decisions you may regret.

Some of your friends may have bad motives. Having fun in the moment is not the only goal. Be aware of what is going on and what will happen as you move forward.

Patience and calmness help you make decisions during important moments. You want to protect your integrity.

Here are some tips to help you when it comes to moderation.

Know how much you can handle.

God doesn't give us more than we can handle, and we have to make good decisions in order to keep moving forward in a positive direction. Good decisions always prove that you are able to handle the freedom.

If you do not have fun responsibly, you will encounter situations which have the potential to put your life in danger. This can happen, for example, when you go to clubs at night. This exposes you to danger.

What would you do if your friend told you to engage in a crime? Any mistake you make in the name of having fun will have consequences.

Create a plan.

Most people have a lot going on, and they need support (with time management skills) for how to behave responsibly. This will helps a person to be accountable to others. Plan for your duties, chores, and all your activities. In the digital age, you don't necessarily need a piece of paper or a physical calendar. Your phone can be used as a reminder when the time for a certain task is done. This enhances responsibility.

When you forget to do your chores, it means you will have to look for another times and opportunities to problem-solve to see how things can be done better next time.

Inspire yourself.

When you are inspired, you are able to go beyond regular ways of doing things.

Work for the community as a volunteer in community cleanup efforts. It will also encourage you to behave more responsibly. Giving to the community will help you see that you have the power to make a difference in other people's lives.

That is why I value Maisha Project. It is an opportunity to become a problem solver and give back so much to the people and place I love.

Learn key life skills.

It is possible to assume that success can come without work. But just because a person is doing well in some areas of life doesn't mean he or she is ready to be responsible in all areas of life. The sure way for people to become responsible is through teaching about life skills on how to overcome the challenges of life and how to communicate with people effectively. When we proactively teach people how to manage time and money and solve problems, it will give them a peace for their minds.

Be clear about cost.

There will be times when we will make mistakes because of poor choices that have negative consequences. If a girl goes to a disco and indulges in alcohol, her judgment will be distorted, and that may lead to having sex with someone. This might then lead to a pregnancy or a sexually transmitted disease. These will change your life. I don't want this for you.

It's disturbing to see people grow up making mistakes that can scar in their entire lives. Even these mistakes can be overcome, but it will put you in a much bigger hole.

Occasional failure is inevitable, but how you overcome it is what matters. And don't quit!

Sometimes in life, you might fall down as many of us have done. But do not remain there. Rise up and walk again. Many young people drop out of school and get involved in drugs and alcohol. Don't follow any peer pressure that leads you that way.

When you realize your mistake, wake up and seek for help. Go back to Luke 15 and read biblical story of the prodigal son who strayed. When he reached a dead end, he made a decision to go back to his father, and he was embraced in a gracious homecoming.

You must get counsel from someone who has more

wisdom than you. I am concerned about the rate of teenage pregnancies in the poverty stricken areas of Africa. This is a major challenge to socioeconomic development because it deprives young girls the opportunity to further their education and attain their career goals.

————

In summary, keeping faith in God during hard times can be extremely difficult. However, I want you to know that not only can our faith grow in times of challenge, but we can discover great joy through trials just like Job did. Tragedy struck, and he lost everything—his children, wealth, livestock, crops, health and even the relationship of his wife and friends. And what did Job do? Not curse God, as Satan had thought he would. Instead, he praised God's name.

The truth is, we cannot redo yesterday, but we can win or lose tomorrow. If we master today and put our best foot forward, we will overcome all odds and rise to greatness. Replace the words "I can't" with "I can." You will succeed regardless of the hurdles that may attempt to use to hinder you. Maintain your current course and avoid looking back; you are on your way to a prosperous conclusion.

In 1 Corinthians 15:58, the apostle Paul writes, *"Therefore, my beloved brothers, be steadfast, immovable, always abounding in the work of the Lord, knowing that in the Lord your labor is not in vain."* This verse is a great reminder that you can make it through. Be steadfast and immovable. Work for the Lord.

Your labor is not in vain! Endurance is only captured through hardship.

Tomorrow is a new day. Whatever happened yesterday or in the past can be dealt with tomorrow. The sun will come up, and it will be a new day, and the rooster will crow to remind you that you have a chance to move forward yet again. You may have gotten knocked down yesterday, but you are strong, you have faith, and you don't quit!

WEALTH-CREATION

"Opportunity dances with those who
are already on the dance floor. So in real
estate, you don't wait to buy, you buy and wait."

—H. Jackson Brown, Jr.

M ost young people have some experience in handling finances. This can come from home, school, or part-time jobs.

However, few of them have any idea about setting financial goals and bigger matters like to saving, earning, budgeting, spending, and investing. I want to spend some time discussing this because it's important to your future no matter where you live or how old you are. Many adults need to hear this too!

The easiest way to become wealthy is to start the journey of wealth creation early. Start with thinking about what type of life and lifestyle you want to live. This vision for the future will help you plan out your steps.

In the stack of learning topics you should be accumulating, add in various books, magazines, and websites about finances. These are helpful tools for you. Watch videos and talks on finances and growing wealth. These may seem boring at first, but they are essential for you to get a handle on all that lies ahead for you if you understand it.

After you get the basics down, you will be more interested in the finer details of retirement funds, money market funds, stocks, shares, treasury bonds, treasury bills, and real estate, etc.

Set financial goals.

It can be tempting to not care about any of this. You want to live carefree and not have to worry about all the things I just mentioned. That may be fun for a bit, but look ahead to the future more. If you don't want to be thirty or forty and in the same situation you are in now, what is going to change? You need to set financial goals.

I have worked with many young people for some time, and I have discovered that people who excel in school and in life set goals and work towards achieving them. This is true in achieving financial success.

What is a goal? It is a pre-determined achievement towards which effort is directed. Goal-setting helps young people obtain clarity on what they seek to achieve including success in financial terms. Any achievement must be created in the mind first before it can be actualized, and that is why goal setting is important.

Financial goal-setting gives you the direction on where to invest and which areas will work for you.

Why is setting goals important?

We live in a world where many things can distract you from pursuing financial success. When you are young, there are many things that you want to do at the same time, and so, if you do not set goals, you will be hijacked by other activities. Successful people learn how to prioritize in order to focus on important activities to achieve their dreams and aspirations.

Goal-setting will also help you identify distractions in order to avoid them. If you do not set clear financial goals, you will most likely get distracted, and you will miss out on a much better, more secure future. Financial goals help you carry out investments that will be in line with your passion and which are workable.

Why do people fail in setting financial goals?

Very few people across the world set goals. The 3 percent who set goals are the ones who are controlling the entire world when it comes to finance and wealth creation. The other 97 percent are waiting for things to become better by themselves without setting goals.

People do not set goals because:

- They lack understanding of the importance of goal-setting.
- They are most familiar with living without setting goals.
- They don't know what they want in life.
- They don't have many opportunities.

Unproductive people believe they have a lot of time on their side, and this makes them want to wait until things are okay to set financial goals.

This is true in Africa, in Oklahoma, and all over the world. There may be reasons why you are stuck, but please don't stay there. Work hard with money, so you can use it for what is good in this world. You can get farther ahead if you will think about this now and as you go forward.

What goals do you have?

Do you have something you'd like to purchase? It could start off being small like a new pair of shoes, or a wonderful dress you've seen, or a gift for your family. It can be something bigger that you would like to save up for and get eventually like a bike or even a car someday. It can be saving for your education or to purchase a home.

All of these goals will take work to achieve. You have to know what you want to do in order to go out and do it. It doesn't just happen.

Monitor self-doubt.

Any time you doubt yourself, you will not be able to set goals. Goal-setting is a statement of a good and true belief in yourself. People who do not believe in themselves will also be easily distracted because they always doubt whether their idea will succeed. Self-doubt leads to fear, and when you have fear, your dreams are paralyzed to the extent that you cannot set goals.

As read this book and as you live your life going forward, do not focus on the mistakes you might have made for not setting goals. This is true in any area that we've been discussing. Take stock of where you are and what you've done, and then move forward in a new direction.

There are always setbacks. You can conquer those and achieve so much. It's possible.

A lack of self-control will get you.

Self-control is a virtue that every person must have. If you do not have self-control, you will not achieve financial freedom because you will not follow your set goals.

Many people have not developed traits that can help them maintain self-control in order to achieve financial success. These traits include determination, strength of mind, and teamwork.

A lack of self-control with money will look like always having an empty bank account and scrambling for money. It can look like an empty pantry or gas tank.

It's not wrong or bad to be poor. God puts us in families, cities, and situations where we do not have as much as other people in the world.

The question is if you are going to work to improve your life not only for yourself but for those who are around you and will come after you. Will you make it better or stay where you are? It's going to take working towards your goals with a determined self-control.

Set your goals successfully.

While this chapter is about financial goals, what follows can apply to any type of goal you might have. You should be setting goals for your money, but also your grades, your projects, your physical fitness, your standards for dating and marriage, and even for your faith.

Successful financial goal setting can be broken into the following acronym—SMART.

S—Specific

You have to be precise in identifying the outcome you want. Clearly defined goals will give clearly defined outcomes.

Thus, don't write down "I want to be happy." That is a great thing to want, but it's difficult to achieve. It would be better to list next what are the things that make you unhappy and work on undoing or avoiding those. And then what does make you happy? That's what you want to work more of into your life.

What are SMART goals for your financial future? These could be to start saving up this month or year for a certain purchase or to have a number in your bank account.

M—Measurable

The goals you make must be something that you can measure. This is because it is impossible to achieve something you cannot measure.

Think about what you want to achieve, but do so in a tangible way. Thus, don't say you want to be rich. That's too vague. Set a specific number you want to work towards for your bank account. Do you want to start with $100? Work through the other steps. Then bump that up to $500 and $1000 as you go ahead.

Or set a time for how fast you want to run a mile. Or a measure for how much you want to weigh. Or what type of degree you wish to attain.

You should know how much you want to achieve. Any goal that is not measurable cannot be scrutinized.

Thus a SMART goal for finances wouldn't be specific or measurable if you wrote down "I want to be rich." That means different things to different people, and it's impossible to measure well. Instead you might say, "I'd like to save $100," or "I want to buy my brother a Christmas present this year," or "I want to own a car." These are specific and measurable goals.

A – Attainable

Set goals that are both realistic and practical, as this will motivate you to pursue them. This can only be done if you are able to appreciate your strengths, and at the same time acknowledge your weaknesses and make plans to address them.

Goals should be somewhat out of reach so that you stretch yourself beyond self-imposed limits, but they should not be out of sight. If you set goals too low, you will not take them seriously, and you could be underutilizing your potential. Develop strategies you can apply daily to achieve the goals set.

Don't forget to make these realistic! While everything is possible, it might be improbable for all of us to set a specific goal of playing in the NBA or becoming a movie star.

For finances, you might not want to start off with a goal of making $1 million. You might get there, but make the first of these attainable. What is realistic for you, both short term and long term?

R– Relevant

Your goals should be relevant. They should help you achieve your overall vision for your life. It is important therefore to attain the knowledge that will enable you to pursue whatever you want to do.

It's good to have a few outlandish or crazy goals, but start with the ones that will most matter to you right now and moving forward.

Financially relevant SMART goals might be to get out of debt, pay off your loans, take a vacation, enroll in a class, etc.

T –Time-bound

Anything you do should factor in how much time it will take to get there. Goals must have timelines by which they should be achieved. This creates urgency so you are able to utilize every available moment. You should not wait for things to be handed over to you.

Goals set should be positive, uplifting, and compelling.

When do you want to pay off your loans or enroll in your class or buy your new phone? That gives you a good timeline to work with.

Get where you want to go.

Think about the person you want to be, and consider how money plays a key part in that future.

Wise people have advised others to:

- Make as much as they can
- Save as much as they can
- Give as much as they can

Make a budget and make a plan. Figure out how much things cost and what it takes to get what you want. Then work as hard as you can. Don't be idle. Find regular jobs and add odd jobs in as you can. Don't waste your money. It can easily slip through your fingers so quickly, and you'll end up with nothing.

Keep track of what you have, so you can know where you've been and what lies ahead. Save up to make your purchases, and try not to live on credit. Save up a little bit, so when thing go wrong or get broken, you can fix them without too much worry.

Be generous. Give a portion (a tithe) to your church, or a charity you believe in. You might start an envelope and put a little money in it every month. As that adds up, notice if there is anyone who needs something that a bit of money might help with. You could give it anonymously, and I promise you you'll feel joy and satisfaction. It might be a piece of clothing, or some food, or an opportunity, or a conference, or a trip. Since you've planned ahead and saved, you will know you can help, and that will be an excellent thing.

Remember that having a ton of money doesn't make you happy. It certainly helps many things, but the Bible teaches us that the love of money is the root of all evil. It can work its way into your heart and cause a lot of damage. Be careful not to love it too much. Use money. Don't let money use you.

Keep your head about you as you make, save, and give.

———

Wealth-creation is simple and easy when done right. As we do business, we create wealth. Not only financial wealth, but also social, cultural, intellectual, and spiritual wealth. Wealth-creation is a godly gift, and God says that he is the one who gives the ability to create wealth. Look up Deuteronomy 8:18.

TIME MANAGEMENT

"Our greatest weakness lies in giving up.
The most certain way to succeed is
always to try just one more time."

—Thomas A. Edison

I want to discuss time management because I think this is a major problem people encounter. They think they have more time than they have. They act like it's unlimited and will never run out.

Time management is how you can control all activities that you take part in within a given time. It's how you can best utilize this resource we've all been given.

If you are still in school, you time is used for studies and academic work. If you have completed your studies, your time would be used for full-time work and preparing yourself for the future.

If you are unwise, your time will be used to sit around. You might take drugs, engage in illicit sexual activities, and participate in things that do not have value for the future. When people do not know how to manage their time, they become frustrated and overwhelmed as they try to do things.

One of the most painful realizations you will have is that you cannot recover wasted time. Time is something that people cannot store to use later. Time-management skills reduce stress and anxiety because you will be able to plan ahead for all your tasks and attend to them in good time. This will save you the consequences of poor time management. You won't lag behind when your peers who managed their time well. You'll see them excel.

When you waste your time in unlawful engagements like doing drugs or crime, you will have conflict with the law of the land. This causes pain and misery in your life and for your parents and family.

When you have control over your time, you will be able to make responsible, efficient, and effective decisions to perform and manage your tasks.

The people who do not manage their time well only attend to tasks that are easy and do not have an impact on their future. They avoid tasks that promote their performance because these require dedication, discipline, and hard work.

You should know that time is quickly passing away, and if

you do not take what you are currently doing seriously, soon it will be too late.

Take each moment as something that is fleeing and must be protected. When you do not understand time management, you will waste your precious time and only try to be busy when what you wanted to do has already taken place.

There is time for everything, and that is why you should prioritize every task. How can you deal with time effectively?

I have a few steps for you to consider.

Set your goals.

When two teams compete, the winner is declared by tallying the goals scored. In the whole affair of time control, goal-setting is key. Goals (we've talked about these before) will help you better manage your time because you will have a clearer direction of where you are going and what you want to achieve in life.

Plan your activities.

Planning helps you overcome the tendency of doing random things. You need specific projects and goals (remember the SMART goals). This does creates a clearer picture of your future which will put you into the trajectory of success.

When you set aside time to plan your tasks, you get better results. Most people who have achieved less than they anticipated have discovered that their lack of planning or inadequate planning was a major contributing factor.

All of your daily tasks should be well planned and done in order of priority or when you are the most productive and alert. Make every effort to ensure that all your must-do tasks are completed within the time allocated for them. You'll feel better and get so much more done.

You can achieve more in your daily tasks by doing the following:

- Set realistic goals for what you want to do during your day, week, month, and year.
- Order your priorities.
- Give each task a number to signify its urgency.
- Manage your time and adjust as you go along.

One trick that often helps people is to set a timer for a task. It can be a bit overwhelming if the task is to clean your room, apartment, or house. But if you set a thirty-minute timer, you can get a lot done in that time and come back to it again later. Another connected idea for this would be to put the whole task into smaller pieces. So in order to clean your room, you might list:

- Wash sheets and make bed
- Vacuum and dust
- Pick up clothes and put them away
- Clear clutter
- Organize desk and closet

Figure out what motivates you best.

Select your tasks.

Most people do not have the patience to do things that are important, especially ones that take longer to finish. They focus on tasks that are easy and take a short time to perform.

Remind yourself that there is always time for important things you need to do. Develop routines and a mindset that will enable you to plan your time well by prioritizing importance and urgency.

Don't postpone tasks.

People who do not perform well keep on postponing what they need to do, hoping to do them later. Hope must be converted into action.

You have to understand the task at hand. Don't underestimate it. It may be difficult and long, but don't wait! Get on it. Go forward.

God has created you with the power to overcome any challenge you might be going through. You can take any huge task and break it down into smaller chunks like we've talked about in this book.

List out the steps that it will take to accomplish what you need. Then focus on the next one. Complete that and move on.

Admit when you fail and move forward.

When you fail to achieve what you set out to do, you have to go back to the drawing board and reflect why you did not meet your goal. It's okay that you didn't get it right from the beginning. No one ever succeeded without failure somewhere along the way. Consider this to be an important learning process, so learn from your mistakes. Don't get discouraged, distracted, or put off. Keep moving forward even if you have had a setback. Tomorrow is a new day to start over!

————

We can learn from the life of Jospeh in the book of Genesis. When his story begins, he is the eleventh son of Jacob. God gave Joseph a dream of his future greatness. God speaks to his children, and he will achieve his will.

Joseph not only dreamed. He understood that God was preparing him for the fulfillment of what God wanted for him.

At Maisha Project, I encourage the young people to be like Joseph. They have to know and then pursue the dreams God has put in their hearts.

God has also chosen you. What are the dreams God has placed on your heart? What purposes will you fulfill as he works through you?

You are uniquely made for a special purpose which God will help you to fulfill. God gives each person a combination of grace, power, self-control, and a purity of heart, body, and soul.

I have seen children who were declared useless by the society grow up to become the Joseph of the community.

In the Psams, we read God say, *"For the LORD God is a sun and shield; The LORD will give grace and glory; No good thing will He withhold from those who walk uprightly"* (Ps. 84:11).

God will give you the power and favor to do outstanding works. I have seen the hand of God working in my life. Every time Beatrice Williamson has felt discouraged because the challenges are insurmountable, I have reminded myself of his promises to me and the assurance of his promises through Christ Jesus.

This assurance has helped me walk in faith, knowing that he is always near whenever I call. My humble prayer is that, as you read this book, God will fill you with the power to achieve great things. Nothing is impossible with God.

Recognize the seasons.

Every new day is a chance to design your future. Don't focus on your past bad days or failures. I know there is a lot of bad news in the world today! We all hear about the latest locust invasion, drought, depression, earthquake, tornado, or pandemic.

I have also seen people starting successful projects and endeavors during this time. We have to press on and move forward.

"Do today what others won't so
tomorrow you can do what others can't."

—Jerry Rice.

As long as you believe in the beauty of your dreams and work hard, your time to harvest will come. Just keep on believing, The most difficult time is right before the victory. So never give up. There will always be tough times.

Eliud Kipchog is one of the world's most prolific marathoners. He amazed the world in one of his many international records because when he was running, the soles of his shoe came out. That did not stop him from pursuing his goal. There was a genuine reason to quit because of the pain of running on his bare feet, but he focused on the main thing, the medal which was at stake.

Don't give up!

There is power in the voice you hear.

When you want to know the source of your success or failure, you only need to do an assessment of the voices that speak to you. Your mind has an incredible power over your success or failure. Your disposition or attitude is determined by the voices that feed your mind. When you train yourself to tune to positive vibration, you will begin to develop the pillars of success.

One of the things that helped me to start my programs was a selectivity of the voices that I allowed into my space.

I have come to the conclusion that everything is possible as long as you have a positive vibration. If you walk with negative people, you will never succeed. If you walk with positive people, you can achieve your dreams. When you change your perception to look at the positive side of things in your life, you will start developing a power to thrive.

When this happens, you no longer dwell on what is wrong because you move into the next phase of finding solutions for how to achieve your dreams. You are a beloved child of God who has the ability to achieve whatever dreams and aspiration you want to achieve and that he allows. Develop a strong wall that will enables you to overcome any negative thing that this merciless world will throw to you.

Fear keeps people from stopping the negative voices. They hate rejection, or they are afraid that they'll ask in the wrong way or say something senseless. Don't fall into fear.

Be thankful.

One of the easiest things to do is to worry, especially when you are faced with uncertainty or an unfortunate situation. This anxiety comes from focusing on the negative rather than the positive.

Many people today don't realize that the reason they're not happy or enjoying life is because they have trained their minds in the wrong direction. They've programmed themselves to worry and complain. They only see the negative.

We can change. We can reprogram our minds to notice and focus on the positive. It all depends on what you think about and meditate on. Discipline yourself to focus on the right things. What is good? What might happen? How can this turn out great? What is God doing in your life because of this?

Live every day like it's your last because one day it will be, and you'll look back on all the things you wish you had done.

When you can't control what's happening, challenge yourself to control the way you respond to what's going on. That's where your power is. Focus on your dreams and desires.

Say no to quitting.

I know this chapter is about time management, but I can't resist to squeeze this in since it's the theme of the whole book.

Do you feel like quitting? I felt like it at various times. I was going through disappointments and experiencing a chain of failure. Sometimes you experience a setback when you are almost at the finishing line. You must press on and fight for your space, so you can win and achieve your dreams.

When I go through down times, I always remember where I came from, and now I give courage, faith, and hope. I know what fear, pain, and distress look like, and I have defeated them through the help of God.

I went through what seemed like endless frustrations and struggles in the slums of Nyalenda. The most important thing I did was not to quit, which would have been easy to do

Remain persistent, reminding yourself that you must continue without complaining until you are fully satisfied with the outcome. Whatever it is that you do, do not quit until you are satisfied. Keep going one step at a time. Keep crossing one obstacle at a time. Each step takes you closer to your destination.

Remain focused on what you want to achieve. There is no time to give up! Keep on keeping on until you become the best of what you were meant to be.

———

In conclusion, time management is another aspect of the concept of balance. It is a most critical aspect of your life if you can instill balance and moderation.

Time management is really activity management because activities are what you plug into the day's time slots. By implementing the strategies, ideas, and tactics contained in this book, you will develop into a master time manager and gain additional time for your work, study, family, and personal life.

Select activities that are the steps toward achieving the most of what God wants you to accomplish for him. Moreover, you will be less stressed, and your work will be completed on time and to a high standard.

Here are more things I want you to know because I believe in you and want you to achieve what God wants for you.

Develop positive relationships with successful people.

If you want to succeed, you have to associate yourself with successful people. If you want to become a great writer, you have to connect with successful writers. They will guide you and give you hidden insights. Seek them out. Contact them. Be where they are.

If you want to be a successful business person, you have to connect with those who have succeeded in those areas. Seek them out. Contact them. Be where they are.

It's true in sports, art, music, computers, engineering,

leadership, and—anything. Seek them out. Contact them. Be where they are.

Successful people don't have fewer problems. They have a determination that nothing will stop them from moving forward. And they get themselves around others who are ahead of them, so they can learn and grow.

Avoid procrastination.

You have to overcome the enemy of procrastination by sticking to your schedule and avoiding distractions (time management!). When you develop your gifts and talents, it will help you to overcome procrastination because sometimes it is brought about by not knowing how things are done. Take your task and break it down into smaller, more manageable chunks. You should also have a way of measuring the progress in pursuing your goals.

Understand who you are.

You have an opportunity to create the future you want, and to do that, you have to know and understand just who you are. It's very difficult to fight an enemy that you don't know. It's also difficult to achieve what you don't know you can achieve.

Do you really understand who you are as a person?

If you have an understanding of your capacity, passion, weaknesses, and opportunities, you will better see where you are going.

Your potential helps to build your character and to achieve the goals and aspirations that you want. Develop an appetite for learning to give you an understanding of things.

In the game of football (soccer in the US), what do you do when the ball is passed to you? You must make a move because the opponent is looking for the same ball to score in your goal. As you make your move, you must focus on the ultimate objective—scoring.

There are many things that are pursuing you as a young person. You must make a move to overcome in order to score in life and have a better life in the future. The game of football or any other game requires that you stick to your game plan. You don't play in the game plan of the other opponent.

Your opponent could be drugs. It could be crime, dropping out of school, teen pregnancy, or poverty. Stick to your game plan so you can find success.

Do you think Tiger Woods just woke up and became the world's greatest golfer? No. He started in as a young person.

If you don't seek knowledge, if you don't develop appositive attitude, if you don't lean and develop your skills, and if you don't emulate the habits of successful people—then you don't have a chance. You must work closely with your mentors to help you harness the greatness that is within you.

I have met many young people who do not know how to get to their potential. They ask me what they should do to achieve greatness. It's a genuine question. It may seem like a mark of ignorance, but it's wise to ask for help from mentors.

Asking is the beginning of learning. Do you know why we do exams? Exams help the teacher gauge whether you have understood a subject or concept.

That's why I encourage you to ask questions in areas you don't understand. As you do, the end will always be better than the beginning.

Why are you not asking questions? Don't try to justify why you don't.

It is because you are full of yourself. You have pride. You have a stubborn unwillingness to admit that you don't know something. The results are disgruntled, weak, and pessimistic people who cannot grow.

It's time to make a decision and get real and get going. Stop trying to cover up. If you are a young person, you must work hard and do what you have to do to achieve your dreams.

Those who become great are the ones that truly understand who they are and what they want to achieve in life.

Only you know what you want to become in life. Just make a resolution—From this day onwards, I resolve to be the best version of me.

God is awaiting to help you discover your gifts and talents. This begins by understanding who you are.

Make a list of what you think are your:

Spiritual Gifts

There are lists in the Bible that tell what types of gifts God gives people. Look through those and ask God to show you yours. Ask others what they think you naturally are drawn to and where they see you are a blessing to others.

Heart

This is a list of what you really care about. Where do your passions lie? What fires you up? What makes you angry?

Abilities

We're not all good at everything. We may have some hidden talents not yet discovered or developed, but the seeds of those might be in there. Others might see them better than we can. Ask.

Personality

Take some tests (you can do this online) to help you think more about what your personality is. Look through the strengths and weaknesses of what you find out. And look at what are positives and negatives of others' personalities. There is no right or wrong. They're all a bit different.

Experiences

This is where you should tell your story and see what comes out. You should include where you are in the birth order, if you know your parents, where you were born and grew up, etc. You should be able to see a few patterns, and it will be interesting to consider how these factors have molded your life. What have you loved? What don't you like?

Notice that these words' first letters spell the word SHAPE. What is your shape?

Understand who you want to become.

What do you want to become as a person? Who are you? What do people say you are?

What you become will always live with you. Young people have a lot of excuses when it comes to digging the foundation of the house of their future. When I look back at where I came from in the poverty and the challenges in the slums of Nyalenda, I can only thank God.

Today, I have supported many vulnerable children. I work to help them have a better life. I lead an important organization. I believe that if I can overcame all these odds, you too have a chance.

You have all you need to be whatever you want to become, but it's not achieved through osmosis. You can't just sit there and expect things to get better.

It takes discipline and hard work to achieve anything. I had to remain focused and determined. Growing is not an automatic process. I had to change my way of thinking to be in sync with what I wanted to become.

I had to learn and break away from toxic friends, some of whom had started abusing drugs and taking part in petty crime. I made a deliberate choice to become different. I learned that, as a young person, you can make a choice and become all you want to be.

Why do most of the young people become unsuccessful Auntie Beatrice?

It is because they do not know who they want to become. So they imitate and follow their friends who also do not know where they are going.

Young people often give up easily when they encounter any type of small resistance. The Mau Mau (Kenya's freedom fighters) fighters knew what they wanted to achieve. The deep understanding of what was at stake created a resilience to fight and achieve the much needed freedom for Kenya.

If you believe in yourself, you will discover your relationships, businesses, inventions, and greatness awaiting you.

Don't settle for less. I am sure you young ladies don't want to become teenage mothers. You boys do not want to be in a rehab because of drugs.

Work on your character.

Be thinking about your future with the seriousness it demands. A fifteen year old now will be thirty in fifteen years from now. That means that today is the only chance you have to design who you will become. And if you don't take today, then tomorrow will be here soon. Will you work tomorrow?

Add value to yourself. Stay motivated and be active in moving toward your dreams. This starts by changing the way you think about yourself. Your mental development is key to designing your future.

Your character will always be important in life. It forms who you are. Decide to be:

- Trustworthy
- Friendly
- Confident
- Loyal
- Kind
- Patient
- Inquisitive
- Thrifty
- Reliable
- Forgiving
- Edifying
- Reverent
- Faithful
- Persistent

Who you want to become can be achieved by simple steps. These are made possible by you!

Your mouth reveals a lot about you.

Your mouth is a key gate through which people can see what is in your heart. When I talk to you, it will reveal to me who you are and what you stand for.

The conflicts and animosities you see in world today are

fights that were triggered by what people say. I hate complaining because every time there is a negative vibration, it affects positive energy. Think about what you say. What comes out of your mouth? Is it encouraging? Does it build others up? Is it truthful? Is it positive?

Don't be a photocopy of someone else.

I have seen many young people who imitate almost everything. When you compare yourself with others, you lose yourself and become a copy. You are unique and different. Your finger prints are not the same as anyone else's.

If you are going to imitate someone, is the person a good role model of what you want to become? Does the person display integrity, kindness, graciousness, truthfulness, and generosity. Imitate people who show you those characteristics.

Empower your mind.

In Maisha Project, I have given a big focus on mindset because it's the place where all the decisions are made. It's where your future is designed. You become what you think. Any success will stem from your mind. You must endeavor to give the best to your mind—books, courses, and the people you associate with.

This has been a constant drumbeat in this book because it's so important.

Be disciplined.

Success is not necessarily a matter of skills. Whatever skills you have take a certain amount of self- discipline. When you are a student or you are on a team, you have discipline to get where you want to go. Self-discipline has the power to convert a dream to greater achievement.

Don't quit!

Work hard.

Remember that most often, the biggest gain comes at the end when others want to quit but you don't.

Have a vision.

Vision is a picture of your future. I shared about the vision that Dr. Martin Luther Kings had for America. He wanted an America where both Blacks and Whites would work together and even play together.

I just spoke of discipline, and that's what it takes to fulfill your vision. *You* have the sole obligation to enlarge your vision.

Your success is in direct connection to your vision.

———

I've covered quite a bit of ground yet again in this chapter. As you work on these, keep in mind that you also need to rest. Build good rest into your schedule each day, week, month, and year. For example, the Bible teaches that Sundays are the Lord's Day, and these are for rest, service to others in mercy, and worship. This is a pattern God sets for us for our good, and it can be difficult to follow!

THE POWER OF ASSOCIATION

"The whole fruit of friendship is in the love itself,
for it is not the advantage, procured through a friend,
but his love itself that gives delight."

—Cicero

The power of association affects your thinking, habits, speech, and activities. It can work for you, and it can work against you. In Proverbs 13:20 we read, *"He who walks with wise men will be wise but the companion of fools will be destroyed."*

To achieve your goals and dreams, collaborate with successful friends and mentors who have different gifts and talents. This will give you opportunities for growth. You can have fun with your friends, but your wider associations will help you with jobs, money, investments, and opportunities for advancement. Who are you going to associate with?

Have you ever had an idea of saving, investing, starting a business, or looking for a job, and you told one of your friends? Instead of encouraging you, they replied, "You only live once" or "Life is too short to bother," and that discouraged you?

Have friends you can have fun with, but pick a different set of people with whom you can talk about big business ideas, the future, and the investment opportunities that are available. It's possible, though it's unusual, to have your friends and these types of acquaintances be the same people.

My advice to young people is to invest in healthy associations because it will enable you to receive feedback regarding behavior, weaknesses, talents, and strengths. You can then use that input to improve and develop yourself. Healthy relationships are important for emotional wellbeing. And that matters in connecting with others freely and sharing experiences that push you and help you grow.

This is a key component to your success. You have to be careful in whom you choose to associate with because they may be key players in your future success or failure. Relationships teach you how to communicate and maintain meaningful bonds with other people.

When you know how to keep strong positive bonds, it takes you to the right path of success. People with healthy relationships are able to share their life achievements and challenges with family members and friends.

What are some of the pointers of a healthy association?

It is a relationship that respects one's uniqueness and allows room for growth and formation of a strong bond. The association is characterized by trust, openness, and honesty. Information is shared freely, and any challenges are addressed without pointing fingers. Differences of opinions are respected and protected. A healthy association has a deep sense of teamwork, thoughtfulness, fairness, inspiration, and support for one another to achieve personal goals.

When you make efforts to cultivate and establish strong bonds, others reciprocate.

Can someone detect an unhealthy association?

People all over the world get trapped in wrong associations. This has caused many deaths and ruined dreams.

Not all relationships are good or lead to your success.

Hear me well. Before you get into any association, you should ask yourself if the relationship is beneficial or if it puts your life in some sort of danger. You should understand all the risks and costs of any association so you can make sensible choices before it is too late.

Unhealthy associations have signs you can look for.

People who are in unhealthy associations are often times

ridiculed and despised. It is a ploy people will use to control the relationship, to manipulate you, and to make you toe the line.

Unhealthy relationships are filled with mistrust. Every step one makes is suspected, and many times, it will be fought and subjected to unnecessary selfish scrutiny. On the other hand, try to see if the trust that is being built might be on shaky grounds. Perhaps this person is asking for a large amount of trust and secrecy, and that could be a warning sign that the relationship isn't equitable and open.

Unhealthy associations are always punctuated by infightings. There will be many disagreements which will lead to bitterness and anger. This is why we have heard of many young people killed in what is described as love-triangle deaths. This happens in part because of the in-fighting among people who they are associating with.

This may be caused by unresolved issues. It is advisable to address issues as they arise within an environment of trust.

When you find yourself stuck in an unhealthy relationship, the best thing for you is to leave. You'll need to best consider how to do that so you will need to consult your mentors and the people who are healthy and seek your best.

People who are in unhealthy relationships will do things out of hate and malice. On the other hand, people in a healthy relationships love each other unconditionally even as they address issues that are problematic. It's not whether or not you have difficult experiences or conversations. It's how you handle them and where they go afterwards.

Mistreatment and intimidation are some of the signs of

an unhealthy association. You can notice this when people are viewed as lesser, weak, invaluable, or stupid. They are often hurt, and their views are disregarded.

Look for and notice any unreasonable demands and favors that will compromise your value system or push you to do something beyond your capability or maturity. This is where people engage in illicit sex and drug abuse because it is demanded by the one who is deemed superior in the relationship.

Unhealthy associations are often characterized by ridicule, embarrassment, abuse, and humiliation. Watch for these in the people you are in relationship. Look for respect, humility, honesty, forgiveness, and kindness.

Seek advice when you feel a relationship is becoming unhealthy. You can talk to your family, teachers, mentors, and friends to help you. Always talk to a trusted person when a situation arises that you don't know how to handle.

Unhealthy relationships should not be ignored because the end will be worse than the beginning. You should also take note that unhealthy associations are not limited to your peers. They can be inflicted by people who are in authority or even relatives.

How do you deal with unhealthy associations?

You have to quit as quickly as possible or else you might pay with your blood and life. You have the power to leave the relationships you engage in. When you realize that you no longer feel a sense of happiness, you have to quit.

When you leave a relationship like this, the best thing to do is to close doors and cut off any links because if you don't, you will end up being hurt again because the revenge element can be ferocious.

Join other groups of people who are having the same passion and vision for what you are doing. This can only be done when you realize your value and worth.

If the situation involves danger, sex, power, or money, be on alert and tell someone immediately. Keep on telling people until you are heard and valued and something happens.

Consider your associations and their trustworthiness.

Be careful about who you trust and associate with. You might trust some people, but you end up being the next topic for gossip. That's a sign that you are in the wrong group.

Before you trust and disclose to someone, ask yourself:

- Does this person genuinely want to help me?
- Do these people have the best interest for me?

You will learn the answer to these questions through watching their actions. The passage of time will can help you know who to trust and who not to.

Listen to their conversations. If they gossip about others to you, it is most likely that they will gossip to others about you.

When they talk about others, are they always discussing

negative things? Because that is the same way they will talk about you.

When you share something with them, it is no longer a secret because a secret can only be with one person.

This shouldn't discourage you from discussing your problems or challenges with close friends, but remember to be careful in selecting who you want to trust with your private information.

———

To summarize, the power of association is enormous. It has an effect on your thought processes, habits, the way you speak, and the things you do.

Who you surround yourself with has a massive impact on your performance and success. The right people will support your efforts and accelerate your success. The wrong people will retard your progress altogether. It is critical that you surround yourself with successful friends and mentors in order to attain your objectives and dreams.

I love this short and powerful verse in 1 Corinthians 15:33: *"Do not be deceived: 'Bad company corrupts good morals.'"*

THE POWER OF COMMUNICATION

"Don't give up on your dreams,
or your dreams will give up on you."

—John Wooden

This current generation is bombarded with all of the information and distraction from social media. This can be a great tool for learning and positive influence, but it can also incredibly negative and harmful. Every time I go to a place where young people gather, they are all glued to their phones or laptops.

The majority of young people spend a significant amount of time on social media. During the pandemic, this only got worse.

Although these platforms can be misused, research has

shown that they can also be used to help people learn, grow, and connect with others. People can now interact with others across the world. Some get work on the other side of the planet.

One of the track stars in Kenya is Julius Yego. He learned his javelin skills on Youtube. After a ton of practice, he applied them on the field and he eventually broke the world record in China in 2015.

You can use social media to help you succeed. There are opportunities out there that did not exist before. When I met Anna Lanson, we would exchange letters. Those took more than six weeks on their way back and forth between Sweden and Kenya.

Today the world is more connected because of the speed of our communication. I can now email thousands of people within an hour, and they reply back immediately.

The benefits of social media.

Social media can help you build a network of new friend-ships, and it can strengthen existing ones.

People who are typically quiet or introverted can feel much more comfortable communicating through social plat-forms. This builds their confidence and enables them to obtain useful information and contacts.

Social media is also used to engage people in programs that are constructive and make a great community. In Maisha Project, I use social media to educate people about our work and also to fundraise for our programs.

Social media has been an effective tool in the dissemination of health related information like the Coronavirus, HIV/AIDS, and other health issues. Social media has also been helpful to encourage people who are usually reluctant to vote to get out and do their civic duty.

There are harmful effects of social media.

Despite the many advantages of social media, it has disadvantages that are harmful to people for social and moral development.

If people want to fit into a group so badly, they can end up losing their grip on themselves. While that is always true in person, it seems even more true online. Think about what people want you to know about them. Is it real? The majority of what people post on their social media platform is an illusion. Things are cropped, framed, and adjusted to give a certain impression.

People share inappropriate photographs, videos, and information to gain popularity. Social media can promote inappropriate relationships between bad and good persons because no one monitors the information exchange.

People can seriously harm their lives by posting things that jeopardize their chances of employment in the future. You must be careful about what you post because whatever you post can be used against you in the future. Employers will check your account, and that will be a factor for hiring you or not.

Social media can be addictive. There are many harmful

sites and people who are out to destroy you. People can easily fall into pornography, gambling, or get caught up in something they never would have expected.

Bullying and shaming are both rampant in the internet. If you become a victim it can trigger depression and result in suicide. Get help quickly, and definitely do not engage in bullying or shaming others.

People can present themselves as authorities when they are only out to hurt you or steal your identity. This is true in security, health, banking, and dating sites. There are many famous examples of people falling in love with a person that didn't actually exist. Sometimes people lose everything.

Be very careful in the use of social media. If you use it responsibly, your chances of becoming successful are higher.

Invest in real people.

While this chapter started with social media, I mostly want to encourage you to invest in real, live people. All of your relationships matter, and social media can help them.

But when everything is on the line, you need someone you can call up who will meet you in your trouble. You need someone who can and will give you a hug or walk with you around the block a few times. You need someone who can look into your eyes and give you hope, tell you the truth, and slap you on the back.

It's amazing that I can be here in Oklahoma City and make a phone call to Kenya at any time. Our technology has made this so wonderful. I can see friends and family. This is so valuable, and I'm so thankful for that.

But I can't touch them. I can't smell them. I can't taste over the screen or phone.

There is something important about actually being there. That's why I try to get to Kenya as often as I can. I need to feel the ground under my feet. I want to taste the spices I love so dearly.

Invest in real, live, flesh and blood people. Don't forsake those right around you so you can live online. While it may be fun to play a basketball video game, go outside and shoot baskets in sun. Get sweaty. Go for a walk. Read a physical book. Start a garden, and learn how to use what you grow to cook good, healthy food.

Real people will be important all throughout your life. If all of your best friends are online, think about how you can make more friends or gain more mentors right where you are.

———

Whether you are a Christian or not, the Bible has some great wisdom on communication. One of my go-to verses is 2 Timothy 3:16, which teaches that *"All Scripture is inspired by God and profitable for teaching, for reproof, for correction, for training in righteousness."* We need important truth in our lives, and the Bible is an excellent source to read and study.

The Bible warns us that what we say and how we say it is important to God. In our world today, social media is either a blessing or a curse (and it can be both in the same minute). However, it is undeniable that it is tough to abstain from. Connecting with others and staying informed has made our lives easier, happier, and more convenient—to some degree.

The challenges of social media may be overcome, and we can move forward with the advancement it has brought to our daily lives. Learn when to put your devices down so you can look at and enjoy the world around you.

THE POWER OF A POSITIVE ATTITUDE

"If you can't fly, then run, if you
can't run then walk, if you can't
walk then crawl, but whatever you
do you have to keep moving forward."

—Martin Luther King, Jr.

Every single day, we encounter both good and bad happenings. These can have a great impact on us and those around us, especially if they are not carefully addressed. They can affect our attitude and lead to repercussions.

Let me give you an illustration. You're eating breakfast with your family, and your daughter accidentally spills coffee on your business shirt.

You have no control over what just happened. What happens next will be determined by how you react to what just transpired. You can get worked up and scold your daughter for spilling coffee on your shirt. She might break down in tears, and then you turn to your anger to her mother and criticize her for placing the cup of coffee too close to the edge of the table.

A short verbal battle might follow before you storm to the bedroom and change the shirt. When you come back to the table, you find your daughter has been too busy crying and unable to finish her finish breakfast. She's not ready for school. She misses the school bus.

Your spouse must leave immediately for work. So you drive your daughter to school. As you speed to school, you are pulled over by the police, and you get a ticket. Because you are delayed for thirty minutes (and charged a fine), you arrive at school one hour late.

When you get to the office, you realize that you did not carry your briefcase.

Your day started badly. As it continues, back home your wife is still offended and has ganged up against you with your daughter. No one wants to talk to you. You fall into bed discouraged and upset.

Why?

Because of how you reacted in the morning.

Why did you have a bad day? Did the coffee cause it? Did your daughter cause it? Did the police officer cause it?

Did you cause it? The answer is **YOU** caused it.

You had no control over what happened with the coffee.

So how you reacted in those five seconds is what changed your day. Your attitude determined your altitude.

You set the pace and direction of how things happens around you. Do not let circumstances set your mood. You do not have to let the negative comments affect you.

React positively, and it will not ruin your day. A negative reaction could result in stress, loss, regret, and perhaps even getting fired from your job if you lose your cool.

I like traveling and adventure. Every year, I invite friends from America to visit my homeland Kenya. This motivated me to start a medical camp, and thousands of the local people have been treated. Lives have been saved.

When you travel for long distances, sometimes storms hit the plane, and you feel uncomfortable and worried. I often felt anxious, especially in my earlier flying experiences. But the pilots always seem to be peaceful and composed. Their attitude is, "We will get there!" We always have.

Growing up on the shores of Lake Victoria in Kisumu, I would occasionally ride in a boat, and there were times I wasn't sure I would arrive safely because of the storms and waves. But the captain was always saying, "It shall be well." We always made it.

You have full control of how you handle and respond to the things that happen in your life. Don't sink the ship. Don't crash the plane. You will make it. You'll get there, and it shall be well.

Your attitude and decisions have a massive outcome on your life. Live your life well. Lay a good foundation of your life with diligence, consistence, and courage. When you encounter limitations, use the challenges, hardships, frustrations, and disappointments to learn lessons. Through your character, patience, hopefulness, and endurance, you will achieve your goal.

We are the pilots of our vessel, and where your end up will depend on the choices you make today. You have to act now. Do not procrastinate. Seize the moment. Grasp your opportunities. When you set your attitude and mindset right, God will work to influence your surroundings and break limitation.

Setting your mindset right by changing your attitude. The moment you conquer your attitude, mind, and perspective, you can shift from mediocrity to greatness.

We are created to be fruitful, rule, multiply, and have dominion. God created us in his own image and likeness. You are the architect of your own destiny and the master of your own fate. You are behind the steering wheel of your life. There are no limitations to what you can do, except what you place on yourself by your own thinking and attitude.

My life has not been smooth. I have gone through hardships, rejection, disappointment, and humiliation. There was a time I almost gave up, but my attitude was too positive to allow me to go down.

I had to discover who Beatrice Williamson was. I had to realize that I am in full control of my life, especially with my attitude about whatever came my way.

God is my mentor. I realized that through discovery there is recovery. If you discover the power in you, and the God you serve has good plans for you, you will recover your lost hope.

It doesn't matter if you grew up in church or haven't had much faith before. God wants to work in your life today.

You may not see how things will work out. All you have to do is believe God. With God, all things are possible! He did not create you to cast you aside. Though you will struggle, you can be a victor. You are strong. You are amazing. God made you, and he loves you. Trust in him. Follow him.

God wouldn't give you the desire to do something without giving you the ability to fulfill it if you are willing and obedient. Wherever there is a will, there is provision.

If you feel life has weighed you down, know that your condition does not represent your position before God. Through God, the ordinary becomes extraordinary.

We all have opportunities to either shrink back and settle or to take a step of faith and embrace all God has in store. God always has a reward for our faith. Stir up your faith. Take a step. Rise and shine for your time of breakthrough, establishment, and harvest.

"Human beings can alter their
destiny by changing their attitude"

—William James

It is good to dream, but it is better to dream *and* work. Desiring is helpful, but desire *and* work are invincible. Everyone has his or her own specific area of influence or mission in life. I love reaching out to help people and change, which is the basis of Maisha Project.

Everyone's task is unique, and you need to find your specific purpose. It's possible to become what you want be. If you want to be successful, it's just this simple—know what you are doing, love what you are doing, and believe in what you are doing. Put a positive attitude in it.

Get rid of mediocrity and focus on a greater purpose. Mediocrity is a serious killer of dreams and destinies. It can turn a president into a beggar. If there is a negative voice in you or around you, you must master it and replace with positive a voice.

Our Almighty God has equipped and empowered you. He has given you creativity, ideas, inventions, skills, and talents. Don't you dare settle for a mediocre life. Remember what the Bible says: *"I can do all things through Christ who strengthens me"* (Phil. 4:13).

No more stagnation. Raise your head high. Don't get stuck in your average performance. Be a leader. Be a hard worker. Set your goals and accomplish them. Ask for help from mentors. Don't settle for average. Be extraordinary!

If you don't want to be average, don't rush into whatever the crowd is doing.

Don't blame others. Take responsibility. People blame everything from their parents to the government for their failure to get ahead in life.

Successful people look at things differently. They refuse to buy into any sort of negative mentality. They make action steps, and they learn new strategies. They look at what is ahead, and they plan to get there.

Don't just sit down complaining and giving excuses. You will get stuck there if you do not take full responsibility of your life. Successful people don't buy into this victim thinking.

There are certain things in life you can't control like the weather, the past, and other people. But there are things you absolutely can control like your thoughts and your actions. Taking 100 percent responsibility for your life is one of the most empowering things you can do for yourself.

But when you live your life on purpose, your main concern is doing the job right. Every day, ask yourself, "Is what I'm doing right now bringing me closer to my destiny?" If it's not, do something that will.

Don't let the past ruin your life. Be willing to go against the tide and say no to what does not matter. There is a seed of greatness in you. You were created to be a victor, to shine, and to partake in God's kingdom blessings.

You are unstoppable, unless you think otherwise. Take responsibility to change a problem into a solution. Decide to live each day like if it's your last day.

Your attitude at the beginning of a difficult task will affect its outcome. God will reward your diligence, and in the end, it's not the years in your life that count. It's the life in your years.

Don't allow negative influences in your life. What seems harmless like a TV show or a negative song can influence your thoughts. Be careful about your choices. They add up over time and what you listen to and meditate on will influence your life more than you would realize.

Spend time building yourself up. Don't waste your time with activities that can tear you down. It often takes wisdom to know the difference, but there are times when it's obvious right away.

Set bigger targets for yourself. Roll up your sleeves, raise your head high, and face life with enthusiasm. Set your mindset right, beat all odds, and go beyond all limits. Be the best version of yourself.

Passion and Choices

Every person hopes to have a bright future and a rewarding career.

However, many learning institutions—especially in Africa—do not really teach young people about career choices. In Africa, this is because the system focuses on exams and not on careers.

Think about what you like to do, are interested in, and are passionate about. What would you do if you had to do it for a whole year or even a decade? What might you pour yourself into?

It's okay if you don't know right away. Keep this thought in mind, and realize it might change. Getting to where you want to go might be easy enough, or it may take years and years of preparation, education, and credentials.

There are influences that impact these thoughts. We may have limited opportunities where we are in our environment. It may be difficult to imagine a career in marine biology if you live in the desert. But look around. This is a good time to consult the internet on what is out there.

Sometimes our parents influence us to follow in their footsteps or conversely to stay far away from what they do. Friends can impact what we think of doing with our lives. Bad friends can steer you toward a career that does not pay well and give you the dignity and fulfillment you deserve.

The grades you score in school will play a big part in how you go forward. Be focused in school so low grades does not become a hindrance to your future.

Young people often select careers because they are more glamorous or are popular with many of their peers. They don't always consider their own personality, talents, skills, and capacity.

If you do not align your career with your gifts and talents, you will discover later in life that the path you ventured into is not aligned with your passions. If you hate seeing blood for example, you cannot make a good doctor. The sight of blood will torment you until the day you quit. It is not in your passion.

What can you do to avoid being entangled in a career that you don't want? This should not happen to any young person in this generation because you have so much information, and there are mentors who can assess your gifts and talents to help you find the right career.

The subjects students choose in school have a direct effect on their future career choices. Choose course that align with your passion and not grades. But make good grades!

Gifts and Talents

Earlier, I shared the story of Eliud Kipchoge, the most revered and fastest marathoner on earth. He identified his gift and talent and worked hard to perfect it. He's made a successful career, and he is sought after to endorse brands.

His slogan is "No human being is limited." That is my point for you too!

You should know yourself, and this will enable you to identify your skills, talents, and personality, all of which play a key role in choosing a fulfilling career. Most successful people have built a career based on their passion. They found what they love doing and activated it to create wealth for themselves.

This includes extracurricular activities outside of your formal education. You might love volunteering at a hospital, taking pictures, or traveling. Think about what you love doing.

Remember though, that there are times when we have to make sacrifices to get there or for the benefit of others. You goal may be postponed, but you'll get to it. Likewise, there might be a job you have to do for pay in order to get to do what you really love until you figure out how to get money from doing it. You may have to work at a store so you can pay your rent and buy your groceries—so you can sing on stage later on in the evening.

Character

You can never walk away from your shadows even when you are annoyed. Your character is a true reflection of who you are, and it contributes a great deal to the career choice you will make.

Your talent can open great doors for you. You may be invited to dine with kings like Eliud Kipchoge has, but your character will determine how long you will stay in that career.

Character helps you determine what is good, bad, desirable, and undesirable. A subset of your character is to determine your values. These are what you think are the most important parts of your life and what you will not give up under any circumstance.

Use this book and others to develop your character, which will play a big part in your greatness and success. We need to constantly gauge our values in line with the careers we want to develop so that we can unlearn unwise values and develop the suitable ones.

In making a career choice, you must be careful to choose something that does not conflict with your values by understanding exactly what you will be doing in this job. Be wary because some careers can compromise the character of a person.

Personality Types

Your temperament helps explain why you act the way you

do. In order to be happy in your career (and life), it is important that you understand your personality type. You need to think about how you are wired, how God made you with your unique personality and story. This affects not only your careers, but your relationships with others.

If you find a career that aligns with your character, gifts, and passion—that is wonderful. Remember that there will be other people in that same field or job, and a part of good work is to get along with others. They've worked hard to get to where they are too. And they have their own unique personality. Look at how personalities work well together and when they clash. Each personality has strengths and weaknesses that we should be aware of, understand, and appreciate.

There are places on the internet where you can learn more about these. This is another good subject to discuss with your family, friends, and mentors.

———

Enriching the mind with positive mental attitudes leads to achievement and progress. Positive thinking keeps your mind healthy and energized. Negative thoughts get stronger as you give in to them.

True positive thinking is not just saying that everything will be okay. You have to be realistic about your losses and setbacks. In order to bring beneficial changes and improvement into your life, a positive attitude has to become your predominant mental attitude throughout the day. It has to turn into a way of life and become a habit. Although this might sound tough, it isn't if you think of it gradual process that is enjoyable.

Remember to focus on the good things, however small they are. If you think of blessings, you will attract blessings. And, likewise, if you think of problems, you will definitely attract problems. Always cultivate a positive attitude and remain optimistic.

If you read the psalms, you will see a range of emotions from those who wrote these amazing poem songs. Look for how so many of them turn to a positive hope in God, even in the midst of tremendously difficult circumstances.

CONCLUSION

I've tried to pass on to you what I would tell you if we had weeks and weeks of time together. I've woven my own life experiences into this advice, and in my next book, I'll tell you even more of my story.

I'm passionate about communicating these truths to you because I want you to succeed. There are so many possible road blocks you might face in your life. Many, if not most, of these have not been ones you've chosen for yourself. However, some of them have been brought about by you and your choices, attitude, friendships, and lack of awareness.

I don't want you to blame your circumstances when in fact you have been lazy, or ungrateful, or too passionate, or not taken responsibility, or not owned up to what you have done.

Remember that we can all learn and grow, and by the grace of God, we can all have a new start in this world.

There is hope! Live by faith. Love God, others, yourself, and even your enemies.

ABOUT MAISHA PROJECT

Maisha Project is an international organization working on local levels to empower people to transform their community. We seek to transform lives and empower communities by providing lasting solutions to address poverty, hunger, disease, and under-education.

We are committed to bringing hope to the hopeless and light to the darkness. Maisha Project began in 2008 through a simple feeding program. It has since grown to serve over 1000 children and community members through education, business opportunities, healthcare, and food security.

Every day, the community we serve faces the risk of disease, malnutrition, and hopelessness. In the Nyanza Province of Kenya where Maisha is located, the silent epidemic of

HIV/AIDS has stolen the lives of mothers, fathers, and children, leaving one out of every three households headed by a child.

According to Kenya's Department of Health, one out of every four adults in the Kisumu district is HIV positive. Breaking generational poverty starts with our children. Maisha resources the existing solution in the communities we serve. Our five-pillar model draws on the power within local communities to break the cycle of poverty. We invest in education, health, local entrepreneurs, missions, and infrastructure community building projects. Sustainability is fostered in all our projects.

To date, over 1000 children have received a life-altering education through our Legacy of Hope project. Over 2.5 million meals have been served to children and families in need of proper nourishment, with over 5000 meals served five days a week.

We continue to care for those living with HIV/AIDS. In 2018, we enhanced health in the community through the service of the Maisha Medical Clinic. We completed construction on our girl's dormitory, soccer field, and other beautification like compound landscaping is still ongoing. Over 850 mission participants have visited Maisha since 2008, with an average of fifty a year visiting the community.

Because of the investments of our wonderful donors, we were able to fund and launch empowerment initiatives like dairy farming and horticulture, as well as additional water projects that will provide clean water. We are committed to have a hopeful, independent, thriving village.

Maisha is the Swahili word for life.

We strive to see a thriving community by taking a holistic approach, bringing transformation, securing sustainability and advancing the Kingdom of God. Each of Maisha's five pillars we view through the lens of

- KINGDOM
- TRANSFORMATION
- SUSTAINABLE
- HOLISTIC

EDUCATION
Shapes the minds of tomorrow's leaders to transform their community and nation.

HEALTH
Secures access to clean water, quality healthcare, improved nutrition and spiritual nourishment.

EMPOWERMENT
Provides small business loans to families and empowers the local staff to initiate community-wide sustainability efforts.

INFRASTRUCTURE
Builds a safe haven for the community and provides the structures necessary to learn, work and play.

MISSIONS

Partners like-minded visitors with local staff to bring support, resources and tools to facilitate lasting solutions for the advancement of the community.

Maisha Project is a registered 501(c)(3) public charity (Tax ID # 46-4992172).
Your donation is tax deductible as allowed by law.
Find us at http://maishaproject.org.

Why Maisha

Maisha Project started with a girl in a small village in Kenya who received sponsorship for education at the age of nine. I am that girl! I founded Maisha to pass on that light and give others the same opportunity for education.

I came to Oklahoma through a ministry exchange program in 2001. When I returned home, I saw change was needed. I knew I had to do something. Opportunities for education were slim for children in my village. They couldn't speak English, which disqualified them from taking the tests required to advance in school. I also saw children drinking from the disease-ridden pool of water behind my mother's house. Many were using that pool as their main water source. They were also going hungry despite the meals my mother was serving from her kitchen each day. Many of my friends and others my age had died of HIV/AIDS or were critically ill, leaving behind orphans to fend for themselves. I knew I had to do something to bring about change.

I began Maisha in 2008, and I'm determined to break the vicious cycle of poverty and enhance the quality of life for every child we serve. I want to empower these children to transform their own community. In addition to meeting physical needs, we also want to meet spiritual needs so that each child has a firm foundation in Jesus. I want the Maisha community to see sustainable change that impacts the future generations of Kenya.

I encourage you to find your own way to make an impact and live on mission, whether that is at Maisha in Kenya or in your own backyard. Through our missions training, so many change agents have been birthed with the desire to impact their own community. I want to encourage you that you really can make a huge impact where you are. With all of us working together, we really can see lasting change in the things that matter most.

———

The Maisha story ignites a passion in all of us to do something! As you engage in serving others, you realize the potential in yourself to create a brighter future, just as I did. We invite you to become a part of the Maisha story.

———

http://maishaproject.org

Discover African Coffee

East Africa is the birthplace of coffee, and the region is cele-brated for producing the most distinctive coffees in the world. Coffee was discovered in Ethiopia, and the country's rich history of vivid floral and fruit forward coffees reign supreme. Kenya began growing coffee commercially in 1889 and, although it produces less than 1 percent of all coffee in the world, it's considered the best you can enjoy.

In the Kenyan coffee farming industry, women own only 1 percent of the land, but they compose 90 percent of the workforce. Although African farmers produce the most cele-brated and in-demand coffee in the world, their labor is not adequately compensated. Global prices are below the cost of production.

Women are disproportionately affected. I grew up in the Nyanza region in Kenya and witnessed this phenomenon first-hand. In Nyanza where I grew up, the main coffee growing area include Kisii, Nyamira, Migori, and Kisumu Counties. The Kisii highlands are agriculturally rich with high and reliable rainfall. The cup profile comes with medium acidity, a body that is smooth and creamy.

Asante Coffee

Welcome to the brilliant world of Asante Coffee.

Asante means "thank you" in Swahili. Every sip and friendly encounter brings you closer to the soul of Africa and the perfect cup of coffee. Asante Coffee has been sourcing green coffee beans from the region where our I was born and raised in Kenya. I started Asante to support the local community, create more jobs for women, and bring a posi-tive part of Kenyan culture to America. I have studied busi-ness administration and wanted to build a brand with strong social values. We are bringing an ethically sourced and high-quality coffee to consumers. My desire is to bring and cele-brate Africa's best products with the world.

From Farm To Cup

Asante Premium Arabica Coffee is grown on temperate slopes in rich red soils in the heart of Africa's Beautiful Highlands regions in Kenya. This Kenya AA Coffee has a reputation as an unsurpassed top-quality coffee. This meticulously prepared East African coffee is famous for its rich body, pleasant, vibrant acidity, and sweet aroma. Hand crafted with love from Kenya, the select coffee beans are hand-picked, washed and sun-dried, then shipped to America as green coffee.

Uhuru Blend is our first blend, and the word *uhuru* means "freedom" in Swahili. With the purchase of this exceptional coffee beans, you are providing economic freedom to our friends from Kenya. Asante Coffee donates 10 percent of its profits to Maisha Project.

Empowering Women Through Coffee

Feel good with a flavorful cup of coffee in the morning and feel better knowing that Asante coffee beans positively impact the women farming them. Asante Coffee is unique in North America. It is single-source, from farm to cup, grown on our own partner farms in East Africa, then it's roasted locally in Oklahoma City and distributed nationally. The result is a brilliant cup of coffee with a perfect balance of body and acidity.

More Than Coffee

Asante Coffee is more than a coffee brand. We believe

that in order to help our country progress, we need to invest in social entrepreneurship opportunities and education. I am determined to break the vicious cycle of poverty to enhance the quality of life for every woman we serve and empower them to transform their community. Take this journey with us to help make a positive impact on the world by simply doing what you love to do every day—drink coffee.

ABOUT THE AUTHOR

Beatrice Williamson is a warm, humorous, distinguished leader and the founder of Maisha Project, a charity whose mission is to see orphans and vulnerable children thrive. It takes a holistic approach to transform lives and empower communities by providing lasting solutions to address poverty, hunger, disease, and education.

She is also an author, motivational speaker, philanthropist, investor, entrepreneur, personal development coach, and co-owner of Becara Realty and Asante Coffee Company.

Beatrice is determined to break the vicious cycle of poverty and enhance the quality of life for every child she serves. In addition to meeting physical needs, "Aunty Bea" (as the Maisha children affectionately call her) is passionate to also meet spiritual needs so that each child has a firm foundation in Jesus Christ.

Beatrice resides in Oklahoma City and holds a Business Administration degree. She travels across the world in speaking engagements.

For additional information, consult the contact page at https://www.maishaproject.org

Or write:
PO Box 444. Oklahoma City, Oklahoma 73101